HANDEL

For Dr Nadine and her Community
– many thanks for arranging
such a grand time for

Hamish

Nov. 1996

OUTSTANDING CHRISTIAN THINKERS

Series Editor: Brian Davies OP

The series offers a range of authoritative studies on people who have made an outstanding contribution to Christian thought and understanding. The series will range across the full spectrum of Christian thought to include Catholic and Protestant thinkers, to cover East and West, historical and contemporary figures. By and large, each volume will focus on a single 'thinker', but occasionally the subject may be a movement or a school of thought.

Brian Davies OP, the Series Editor, is Regent of Studies at Blackfriars, Oxford, where he also teaches philosophy. He is a member of the Theology Faculty at the University of Oxford and tutor at St Benet's Hall, Oxford. He has lectured regularly at the University of Bristol, Fordham University, New York, and the Beda College, Rome. He is Reviews Editor of *New Blackfriars*. His previous publications include: *An Introduction to the Philosophy of Religion* (OUP, 1982); *Thinking about God* (Geoffrey Chapman, 1985); and he was editor of *Language, Meaning and God* (Geoffrey Chapman, 1987).

Books already published in the series:

Anselm	**Handel**	**The Apostolic Fathers**
G. R. Evans	Hamish Swanston	Simon Tugwell OP
Denys the Areopagite	**Yves Congar**	**The Venerable Bede**
Andrew Louth	Aidan Nichols OP	Benedicta Ward SLG
Reinhold Niebuhr		
Kenneth Durkin		

Planned titles in the series include:

Berkeley	**Teresa of Avila**
David Berman	Rowan Williams

HANDEL

Hamish Swanston

GEOFFREY
CHAPMAN

Geoffrey Chapman
An imprint of Cassell Publishers Limited
Villiers House, 41/47 Strand, London WC2N 5JE, England

First published 1990

British Library Cataloguing in Publication Data
Swanston, Hamish, *1933–*
Handel. — (Outstanding Christian thinkers).
1. English music. Handel, George Frideric, 1685–1759
I. Title II. Series
780.92

ISBN 0–225–66598–0 (hardback)
0–225–66595–6 (paperback)

Typeset by Colset Private Limited, Singapore
Printed and bound in Great Britain by
Biddles Ltd, Guildford and King's Lynn

Contents

Editorial foreword

St Anselm of Canterbury once described himself as someone with faith seeking understanding. In words addressed to God he says 'I long to understand in some degree thy truth, which my heart believes and loves. For I do not seek to understand that I may believe, but I believe in order to understand.'

And this is what Christians have always inevitably said, either explicitly or implicitly. Christianity rests on faith, but it also has content. It teaches and proclaims a distinctive and challenging view of reality. It naturally encourages reflection. It is something to think about; something about which one might even have second thoughts.

But what have the greatest Christian thinkers said? And is it worth saying? Does it engage with modern problems? Does it provide us with a vision to live by? Does it make sense? Can it be preached? Is it believable?

This series originates with questions like these in mind. Written by experts, it aims to provide clear, authoritative and critical accounts of outstanding Christian writers from New Testament times to the present. It will range across the full spectrum of Christian thought to include Catholic and Protestant thinkers, thinkers from East and West, thinkers ancient, mediaeval and modern.

The series draws on the best scholarship currently available; so it will interest all with a professional concern for the history of Christian ideas. But contributors will also be writing for general readers who have little or no previous knowledge of the subjects to be dealt with. Volumes to appear should therefore prove helpful at a popular as well as an academic level. For the most part they will be devoted to a single thinker, but occasionally the subject will be a movement or a school of thought.

The subject of this volume may seem a curious candidate for the title 'Outstanding Christian Thinker', for Handel was no professional theologian and wrote no theological treatise. But, as Hamish Swanston argues with wit and originality, he explored the religious significance of narrative so as to make ordinary Christians of his time more aware of the significance of Scripture for them. By studying Handel's career and its context, and by looking especially at his shaping of the oratorio, Professor Swanston shows how one can find in his work a theology expressed in musical idiom. He suggests that through his retellings in his operas of a series of romantic tales, histories and myths, Handel equipped himself to declare the reference of the scriptural narratives to the lives of his contemporaries. He also shows how, in his later oratorios, Handel offered a way forward for Christian thinking after the aridities of early eighteenth-century argument.

Brian Davies OP

Preface

On Sunday evenings when my mother was a little girl, almost a hundred years ago now, tea having been cleared away, her grandfather would sit down at the organ that he had himself built in the parlour to play a selection of airs and choruses from Handel's oratorios. It was not a big instrument, but big enough for its noise to fill the house. 'Hallelujah' sounded very loud.

She was being introduced to a tradition of Handel that made a catena of Sir John Hawkins' notice of the aged composer's church-going, his charity performances of the oratorios for the poor prisoners of Dublin, John Wesley's testimony to the 'ever so serious' congregation at a Bristol *Messiah*, the 'funeral march' from *Saul*, Johann Graupner's choral society in Boston, Massachusetts, the Three Choirs Festival, and the artisan's Sunday recreation. But even as the old cabinet-maker and his grand-daughter sang in the parlour, Bernard Shaw was making his protest against 'the church-going mood' of English performances of Handel's works. 'We get broken in to the custom of singing Handel as if he meant nothing' when it should be apparent that he was 'tremendously in earnest' and 'meant a great deal'.[1]

Shaw himself never got round to saying quite what it was that he thought Handel meant. And to some critics it now appears impossible to discover Handel's view of the great matters of human debate. Remarking that whilst 'we can document Handel's public and professional life with fulness and precision', Donald Burrows laments that 'we know virtually nothing about his opinions on the political, religious or philosophical issues of his day'.[2] There is, indeed, very little evidence of those sorts of opinion in the great collection of historical records, contemporary references and personal reminiscences, published by Otto Erich Deutsch as *Handel: a Documentary Biography*.[3] But the recovery of a creative artist's understanding of experience, even if such personal papers were abundantly available, could only be attempted through attention to the artist's works.

Handel was 'tremendously in earnest' not only about the practicalities of dramatic story-telling but about the reference of the stories he was telling. The romantic yarns, the historical melodramas, the mythic fantasies that his librettists provided, should bear upon contemporary living. It is as necessary now as in April 1737, when the *London Daily Post* was advising its readers 'to carry a Heart for the Sense as well as an Ear for the Sound', in order to discern what Handel meant. He took for himself the sole proprietorship of the texts. From the complaint of Rossi in 1711 that 'the Orpheus of our century' had scarcely given him time to write a quick libretto for *Rinaldo*, through Jennens' irritation at the composer's head being 'more full of maggots than ever' as he thought of new ideas for *Messiah* in 1738, to Morell's wry amusement at having to alter his iambics into trochees for *Theodora* in 1750, the tale of Handel's relations with his wordsmiths is of one kind: 'No', he said, 'I will have this'.[4]

Along with that settled determination to control the sense of his story, Handel exhibits, through the great sequence of operas and oratorios, a developing consideration of himself, of the world he inhabited, and of God. His boyhood experience of the Pietist community in Halle had given him an appreciation of the Christian dignity of a layman's conversation and a layman's music. He dealt familiarly with the scapegrace Lutheran theological student who wrote an opera libretto for him in Hamburg, and the civilizedly encouraging cardinals in Rome, who confirmed his sense of being at his ease in scriptural and theological discussion. His relations with English clerical text-makers, like Morell and Miller and even the more learned Broughton, are less dramatic but no less significant instances of his mature assumption of a theological competence than his tart response on the Archbishop of Canterbury's sending him the texts for the 1727 Coronation Anthems: 'I have read my Bible very well, and shall choose for myself'.

There is some real interest in an admirer's recollection of the assiduity of Handel's attendance during his last years at the services of St George's, Hanover Square. But more may be learnt, I think, of Handel's mind from a chronological viewing of his work and its contexts, making a start with the music he heard as a boy and the music he wrote as a young man at the Hamburg theatre and in the courts of Italy, and continuing with reference to the changing topics of British divinity during his years in London.

It took him a quarter of a century after the Coronation of 1727 to turn that scriptural competence to creative theological account. A quarter of a century of discovering opportunities and talents, of reconsidering the varieties of dramatic narrative, of clearing away his own and others' misconceptions of what was important in Christianity. He did not come suddenly upon the wonder of his retelling of *Jephtha*.

Unsettled by missionaries, traders and seamen, who brought home tales of foreign godlings, irritated by the suggestions of comparative religionists, and not wishing to encourage deist criticism of the Hebrew and Christian Scriptures, Georgian theologians were generally agreed in dismissing the narrative forms of the Bible as irrelevant to the doctrinal content. In this context, Handel's London operas and oratorios may be appreciated as counter-demonstrations of story-telling as the proper way to do theology. What the divines had been saying about mystery and myth and revelation, about self and liberation, comes together differently within the structure of Handel's story-tellings. Not for members of his eighteenth-century theatre audiences only, but for the Victorians singing in the parlour, and for us, Handel becomes a forwarder of Christian thinking.

Notes

1   G. B. Shaw, *Music in London* (21 January 1891). The history of this 'church-going mood' is nicely set down in *Handel's Dramatic Oratorios and Masques* (1959) by Winton Dean, the most learned of modern Handel scholars.
2   D. Burrows, 'Handel: his life and work' in J. Simon (ed.), *Handel, A Celebration of his Life and Times*, catalogue for a National Portrait Gallery exhibition (1985), p. 9a.
3   All otherwise unreferenced biographical material quoted here, including excerpts from J. Mainwaring, *Memoirs of the Life of the Late George Frederic Handel* (1760), is to be found, with its original sources, at its chronological place in that absolutely indispensable collection (1955).
4   Datings of cantatas, operas and oratorios refer throughout to first performances. I have gratefully relied, for that order of fact, on the indefatigable scholarship of Anthony Hicks' Work-list in the new edn of Sir George Grove (ed.), *Dictionary of Music and Musicians*, ed. S. Sadie (1980), together with W. Dean, *op. cit.*, and W. Dean and J. M. Knapp, *Handel's Operas, 1704–1726* (1987).

1

Beginnings

The young Saxon among Halle Pietists
and Roman cardinals

As with Shakespeare, so with Handel. There is no record of his birth. Only the day of his baptism is registered at the Lutheran Liebfrauenkirche in Halle-on-Salle in Upper Saxony. He was baptized Georg Friederich on Tuesday, 24 February 1685. His father had settled in Halle after service as a surgeon in the Thirty Years War. Dr Händel was over 60 years old, with grown-up daughters and grown-up sons, when he married his second wife, Dorothea Taust, on St George's Day, 1683. Handel was their only son to survive infancy.

The surgeon's father had worked his way as a coppersmith from Breslau to the more congenially Protestant jurisdiction of the Elector of Saxony. The family of Handel's other grandfather had also migrated from Habsburg territory in hopes of evangelical contentment. Dorothea Taust's father was the Lutheran pastor of Giebichstein and Crollwitz near Halle.

Not much was known to John Mainwaring (1724–1807), the composer's first biographer, of Handel's childhood, and little more has been learnt since this Cambridge Professor of Divinity published his account in 1760. Handel may have been sent to the local Stadtgymnasium, but it is more likely that he was placed at a Lutheran school in Halle, founded by the great Pietist August Hermann Francke (1663–1727). Francke's curriculum for the burghers' children consisted of religious instruction, reading, writing, arithmetic and music. His Paedagogium flourished despite resentment amongst the local clergy. Francke was rather too insistent for most of them on the inspiration of lay women and men in the Church, and on the primacy of personal devotion over the clergy's pulpit sermons and sacramental liturgies. He

1

and his fellow Pietists at Halle, Christian Thomasius (1655–1728) and Justus Breithaupt (1658–1732), for example, were much more ecumenically minded than most contemporary Protestants, and their accounts of orthodoxy gave ample scope for the beliefs of Roman Catholics, Reformed Calvinists and the more radical Christian sects, as well as for the varieties of their Lutheran fellows. The origins of Handel's cheerful confidence in dealing with a wide range of Christian believers may be sought in the teaching and example of these Halle pastors.

Pietist distrust of ecclesiastical establishments prompted a non-liturgical Christian music. Philipp Jacob Spener (1635–1705), the Alsatian founder of German Pietism, and several of his followers, wrote verses designed to be sung in the parlour, on the farm wagon, and at the community picnic. Francke's people were especially songful. They were ecumenical in their music, too. With their own new hymns, they sang the old songs of the Bohemian Brethren, and the verses brought from France to Halle by immigrant Huguenot glass-blowers who were settling there in large numbers, all through Handel's boyhood, after the revocation of the Edict of Nantes in 1685. They were equally pleased to make music for a number of the poems of mediaeval Catholic mystics. By 1705 there were enough of these laypeople's hymns to be collected into a Halle songbook. Convinced, as Johann Anastasius Freylinghausen (1670–1739) affirmed in his preface to this *Geistreiches Gesangbuch*, that God 'has placed a new song in the hearts and mouths of his children', and that 'He uses Christian hymns and canticles to move men's hearts' as they go about their usual business, they had hymns for every occasion.

It may be that the awfulness of many of the verses sung in the Halle community convinced the young Handel that a composer should retain for himself a total command of whatever text a librettist offered him. Certainly, his lifetime debt to the Halle Pietists should be assumed to include preservation from the clerical notion that the liturgical anthem in the church is the only fit setting of the scriptural text.

Reading that text at home, the Pietists discovered, in certain words and pericopes, some especially emphatic declarations of God which command the particular attention of the Christian. It was not until 1724 that Johann Jacob Rambach (1693–1735) formalized the practice of such reading in his *Institutiones hermeneuticae sacrae*, but the Halle dominie had been exercising this discernment of spiritual emphases when Handel was a schoolboy. All his life, Handel was to maintain a like approach to the texts that librettists provided for opera and oratorio, placing his musical emphases whenever his imagination was seized by a word or phrase. '*Comfort* ye' and 'I *know* that my

Redeemer liveth' were common Halle examples.

Organ-loft to opera house

Having two daughters married to doctors and two sons doctors themselves, Dr Händel destined his youngest boy for a career in the law courts. But Handel's own talent, the encouragement of Duke Johann Adolf I, who, Mainwaring reports, heard the youngster play on the organ of his chapel at Weissenfels, and the general opinion of the old doctor's friends, conspired to persuade him that Handel should be allowed to study with Friedrich Wilhelm Zachow (1663–1712), the distinguished organist of the Marienkirche in Halle. Father and mother may have thought Handel's becoming a decent cathedral organist or Kapellmeister almost acceptable as an alternative to his attaining some legal eminence. When, however, the doctor died in 1697, there remained some doubt about Handel's future. In February 1702, the seventeen-year-old registered as a student at Halle university without specifying the course of studies he meant to follow. By March that year he had got himself appointed, for a 'probationary' year, as organist at the Domkirche. The Calvinist elders needed someone to play on Sundays and feast days, to 'pre-intone the prescribed Psalms and Spiritual Songs', to provide the congregation with 'the support of beautiful harmony' on the organ, and to keep the instrument itself in good repair.

There was probably nothing personal in the appointment being for just one year in the first instance. The elders had had to fire Handel's predecessor for failing to 'lead a Christian and edifying life'. It may have been, since they had already employed the young man as deputy to the dismissed Leporin and had been pleased with his music and his manners, that the Calvinists were not yet quite sure that they should give a permanent cathedral appointment to a Lutheran sprig.

The probationary year ended with Handel himself determining to quit Halle and try how far his music might get him in the great city of Hamburg. There, clambering about the organ-loft of the Magdalenakirche on 9 July 1703, he met the young singer and composer Johann Mattheson (1681–1764). Mattheson was enthusiastic for all sorts of music; he was to set out a fine 'defence of opera' in his *Untersuchung der Singspiel*, but at the time he was prospecting for the job of organist at the Marienkirche at Lübeck. Handel went auditioning with him in August 1703. Bach may well have been looking for the same post when he went to Lübeck in 1705. None of them got it. Mattheson and Handel, but not the more civilized Bach, put about the ungallant story of not wanting to fulfil the condition of marrying Margreta Buxtehude, the retiring organist's daughter. The two young friends went back to work for the opera house in Hamburg's Gänsemarkt.

Handel was first employed as a second violin player, and then, in December 1704, he was promoted to lead the orchestra from the harpsichord for performances of Mattheson's *Cleopatra*, in which the composer himself was singing Antonius.

Mattheson may have chosen this Roman piece in hopes of repeating the success with Hamburg audiences the year before of a *Claudius* opera by Reinhard Keiser (1674–1739). Keiser, the director of the company for the whole of Handel's Hamburg years, was the composer of at least 100 operas. He tackled Roman history again the next year with *Lucretia* and *Octavia*, but was ready to write music for as many sorts of plot as Polonius discovered the Wittenberg players to have in their repertory: biblical pieces like the *Salomon* of 1703 and the *Nebucadnezar* of 1704, mythological extravaganzas like the *Venus and Adonis* of 1697 and the *Orpheus* of 1709, historical romances like *Masagniello furioso* (1706) and *Almira, Königin von Castilien* (1704). Keiser could not restrain his lively talent for tune-making. His operas were always too long, and shapeless. He was careless of plot and character. But then, Heinrich Hinsch, his librettist for *Der verführte Claudius*, had located the pleasure of opera precisely in 'the total absence of anything that makes a demand on the reason or understanding'. No one in Hamburg seems to have worried much about opera as story-telling.[1]

Anecdotes of Handel's grandfather's journeying into exile, his father's famous tale of his operating on the boy with the knife in his throat, and his half-brother's gossip from the Weissenfels court provided diverse examples of how to tell a story. In London, Handel himself was known as a skilful raconteur, though not everyone at the supper table could follow as he jumped between the German, Italian, French and English phrases of his stories. As a young man in the Gänsemarkt, however, he recognized that, whatever he knew about story-telling, he had a great deal to learn about making operas. He followed Keiser's example and concentrated on making lots of tunes for a plot as it meandered from incident to incident. He made an *Almira* opera. Keiser generously put it on during January 1705.

Almira slips from comedy to tragedy and back with little to hold the action together except the ballet between scenes. At its close, the Spanish princess who is its heroine discovers that, amongst all her suitors, the man she loves had, as a baby, been picked up by

4

fishermen, and is truly a marriageable nobleman. All this is musicked in a dozen different fashions. There are even hints of Zachow's cantatas. These may have pleased Friedrich Feustking (c. 1678–1739), the first and least respectable of all Handel's clergymen librettists. *Almira* was just the sort of thing that Hamburg audiences had been trained to like. Mainwaring says that 'the success of it was so great' that it ran for 30 performances without interruption. Mattheson, reading this account, indignantly corrected it to 20 nights.

Handel was to write a great number of such romances about love, honour, and the confusions of aristocratic affairs, but during the run of *Almira* he was spending his days writing that other sort of Keiser opera by which Mattheson had himself hoped to achieve a fame. He was composing the Roman tragedy *Nero*.

Nothing survives of the music for *Nero*. Probably it was all thrown into the wastepaper basket after the fiasco of its two-night run. Handel would attempt the subject again, but for now he was quick to put aside this Roman history failure, and sit down to compose what turned out to be an immensely long, two-opera version of a Greek myth. The first opera, *Florindo*, is a tale of the lordly Apollo who, being hit by Cupid's dart, falls in love with Daphne, a nymph already promised to the shepherd boy Florindo. The complications thus established continue into the second opera. At the catastrophe of *Daphne*, the nymph is turned into a laurel tree, the sun god is forced to acknowledge that love is a greater god than he, and the shepherd makes do with a second-best mate. Handel was to return several times to this story of Apollo and Daphne.

Almira, *Nero* and the two-opera *Florindo–Daphne* constitute an exemplary sequence of topics for early eighteenth-century composers of opera. They were all writing such things. Handel's music is not especially distinguished yet; it declares his delight in Frenchified fashions and Italianesque mannerisms, but with a rather Hamburger stiffness. There are, however, signs that he is working out for himself how individual incidents might be brought within a coadunating design. He is already more sensitive than Keiser to the places in a text at which the emotional charge of a whole scene may be communicated to an audience. He is beginning to appreciate the possibilities of the Italian aria as an indicator of both the critical moment of an opera's action and the individuating response of a character to what is going forward in the action. These operas are to be noted as Handel's first efforts towards that mastery of romantic tales of love and honour, classical histories, and the larger wonders of mythic narrative, later exhibited in *Orlando*, *Giulio Cesare in Egitto* and *Hercules*. He had not yet tried his hand at imitating Keiser's biblical music.

Among his audience at one of the spring 1705 performances of *Almira* sat the Most Serene Prince Ferdinando de' Medici (1663–1713), elder son of the Grand Duke Cosimo III of Tuscany, and one of the half-dozen truly civilized members of the prolific Florentine dynasty. Mainwaring suggests that composer and prince 'frequently discoursed together on the state of Music in general, Singers and Performers in particular', and that in this friendly gossip, the prince proposed that Handel journey to Italy 'to reconcile him to the style and taste which prevaileth there'. Handel had already determined on a journey to Italy, but he wanted to go, as Mainwaring also says, 'on his own bottom'.

It had never been, he told the unfortunate manager of the theatre, his intention to settle down in the Hamburg orchestra pit. 'He came thither only as a traveller, with a view to improvement.' He was now resolved to see what was happening in the world 'before he entered into any engagements which would confine him long to any particular place'. Leaving the Hamburg company to make what they would of *Florindo*, Handel set off for Rome.

From opera to oratorio

Handel several times reused music from *Almira*, so it is possible that he packed a conductor's score in his portmanteaux, but a more manageable calling-card would have been the *Laudate pueri* for soprano, two violins and continuo, which is the oldest Handel autograph MS extant. He may have composed cantatas for the Halle Lutherans whilst he was studying with Zachow. There is no sign of these now, nor of anything he may have written during his Domkirche year with the Calvinists. But Handel was very well aware of the Church as patron as he made his plans for Italy. Perhaps he abandoned *Florindo* because it could not serve his purposes in Rome, where public performances of opera were forbidden.

It is very likely that Handel stopped at the Medici court on his way to Rome. Florentine cultural life was no longer dominated by the sober sense of duty encouraged by the example of Cosimo *Il Vecchio*, but then it never had been since the younger branch of the family had taken over the governance of the city and set their minds on being created Grand Dukes. The Most Serene Ferdinando, his uncle Cardinal Francesco Maria and, in a lesser way, his brother Gian Gastone, kept a lively and innovative sense of the beautiful going in their villas outside the city. But any expectation that Handel had of a bright, cheerful, art-loving and fun-loving court would have been disappointed. The Grand Duke had in old age become inquisitorially strict in the supervision of his subjects, forbidding Tuscan students to attend universities outside his demesne lest they come upon heretical teachers, suppressing the folk songs of May Day as relics of mediaeval paganism, and rebuking their mercantile fervour as he went on foot to the shrines of canonized Florentines, where he prayed for the conversion of Protestant guests at his court. Handel did not delay long in Florence. He wanted to try the grander opportunities of Rome.

Francesco Valesio notes in his *Diario di Roma* for 14 January 1707 that the latest sensation was a *sassone* who had been giving 'a flourish of his skill' on the organ of San Giovanni. The young Saxon was quickly taken up by a group of distinguished friends, Cardinals Pamphilj, Ottoboni and Colonna, and the Marchese Ruspoli.

Benedetto Pamphilj (1653–1730) was the oldest of these patrons; a gentleman poet much amused by words and ways of convoluting them into Baroque verse. He could produce an impromptu rhyme of some wit and charm, even composing a few stanzas as a delicate compliment to the young musician, 'Handel, my muse cannot manage to sing', which Handel, equally game, at once set to music. More interesting than 'Hendel no può mia Musa' was Handel's setting of Pamphilj's oratorio text, *Il Trionfo del Tempo e del Disinganno*, performed at one of Ottoboni's Lenten concerts in 1707. Opera being banned, the cardinals could sit with a clear conscience to hear Time and Truth triumph over Pleasure.

'Oratorio' had its origin in the music of the Roman Oratory, founded by St Philip Neri (1519–95) in 1564. The singing of *laudi spirituales*, religious songs in the vernacular, was as essential a part of the Oratorians' apostolate among the bright young men of Rome as it had been of the Pietists' mission to the artisans of Halle. The Oratorians took the best of the tunes they heard being whistled on the streets, sometimes fitting them with new religious verses, sometimes altering the sentiments by judicious censorship of a few phrases, sometimes simply supplanting the name of the songster's beloved by 'Maria', and told the boys to go on singing. From these beginnings the form of the oratorio was developed at meetings of the lay Brothers of the Oratory. Alongside the conversion of popular songs there was a gradual conversion of the secular cantata to holy use. It was in 1600, the very year when opera was invented for the Florentine court, that the first recognizable oratorio, *La Rappresentazione di Anima e di Corpo* by Emilio de' Cavalieri (c. 1550–1602), was performed at the Chiesa Nuova. But it was not until the middle of the seventeenth century that 'oratorio' was applied to a concert work.

It is not clear, when he undertook Pamphilj's commission, what Handel knew of the oratorio tradition in Italy. Perhaps the conversation round the cardinal's table included anecdotes of the 1638 Palermo production of *Sansone*, or the 1651 *Debbora* at Ancona. There may have been some at the palazzo who had attended the 1695 performances of an *Ester* by Alessandro Stradella (1638–82) in Bologna. It is not clear, either, how much Handel knew of the Latin works of Giacomo Carissimi (1605–74), who had developed for the Jesuits a more deliberately apologetic and emotionally compelling form of oratorio performance. Certainly, Handel retained in London some memory of Carissimi's treatment of the Solomon and Belshazzar stories, and he showed by various references in his own music a continuing enthusiasm for the Roman oratorio Carissimi made in 1650 from the Jephthah narrative.

The *oratorio volgare*, with its Italian rather than Latin text, had, by the time Handel arrived in Rome, become a Lenten tradition, Alessandro Scarlatti (1660–1725) having proved how entirely a great composer could accommodate theatrical music within the conditions of the papal ban on opera. He had written a number of oratorios telling biblical stories, but Pamphilj's libretto for *Il Trionfo* was designed after the example of Scarlatti's allegorical dialogues. Ottoboni provided not only a quite large number of players for Handel's orchestra, but four really capable singers. He delighted in exploiting these resources. The quartet in which Time, Truth and Pleasure demand that Beauty decide which of them she will trust is splendidly managed towards the irresistible moment when Beauty realizes what she must expect at the hands of Time.

Handel was happy enough with the piece to bring it into his London repertory 30 years later, carefully remedying some mistakes in his youthful accentuation of the Italian language. He tried out another revision twenty years on from this, engaging Thomas Morell (1703–84) to make a translation of the libretto, but this 1757 Englishing was not a success. The new words just would not fit the rhythms of the music. *Il Trionfo* is an entirely Italian work. In Hamburg Handel had himself attributed the failure of *Nero* to a lack of spirit in the German verse: 'one feels vexation at setting such a thing to music'. Now in Rome, recognizing how awkwardly he had stretched and crammed the Latin of Psalm 112, he was composing a new *Laudate pueri*. Retaining total command was already being understood by Handel to entail his responsibility for the sense of the words.

Pietro Ottoboni (1667–1740), who paid for the production of *Il Trionfo*, was the most generous of the three cardinals, a lavish patron of musicians and artists, and thus an accumulator of vast debts. In

1707 he held musical parties in his Palazzo della Cancelleria every Monday that he was in Rome, liturgical season permitting. There was almost year-round employment for his band and its leader, Arcangelo Corelli (1653–1713). Perhaps the greatest violinist of his age, Corelli is said to have endured advice from the Saxon second fiddler during rehearsals of *Il Trionfo*.

Carlo Colonna (1665–1739) is associated with a more liturgical project for the summer of 1707. When the Carmelites under his protection celebrated their feast of Our Lady of Mount Carmel in Santa Maria di Monte Santo on 16 July, it was Colonna's habit to pay for the music. In 1707 he commissioned settings of the *Laudate pueri* and *Nisi Dominus* psalms from Handel for Solemn Vespers of the feast.[2] The choir may also have sung his startlingly devotional *Salve Regina* at the close of the celebration, but this had first been performed a month before at the Vignanello castle of the Ruspoli family during festivities in honour of St Anthony of Padua.

In 1706 the Marchese Francesco Maria Ruspoli had inherited rich estates at Vignanello and Cerveteri, and he was anxious to obtain some proper public acknowledgement of his new importance. He needed an inventive composer and a splendid title. It took until February 1709 for the Marchese to be elevated by the Pope as Prince of Cerveteri, but by May 1707 Handel was installed at his palazzo composing cantatas for the fashionable diva Margarita Durastanti to sing at *conversazione* on Sunday evenings. Among the hundred or so cantatas there are many anticipations of future achievement. The famous *Armida abbandonata*, for instance, is a sketch for the complex relation of enchantress and Christian knight worked out in *Rinaldo* and *Alcina*. And in *Agrippina condotta a morire* there is a promise of Handel's command of a more inward drama. The psychological distress of Nero's mother as she is led to her death is mirrored in the breakdown of the cantata form. The disintegrating mind is known in the sudden changes of *tempi*, in the abrupt shifts between aria and recitative, in the sudden silence at the end. This is a Baroque music: aggressively synaesthetic; as determinedly breaking down the divisions of sense from sense as the floating stone draperies of Bernini's St Teresa in the Cornaro chapel. Or the gesticulating Aeneas of Pietro da Cortona's ceiling for the long gallery of Pamphilj's palazzo in the Piazza Navona where *Il Trionfo* was first performed.

After this exciting return to the scene of *Nero*, it might be expected that Handel would take an opportunity to write something of the mythic, *Florindo*, world. Pamphilj, Ottoboni and Ruspoli were, after all, members of an Accademia Arcadiana. It was at a summer picnic of this mock-pastoral club that Pamphilj versified his instantaneous praise of Handel as *novello Orfeo*, a new Orpheus. And Handel wrote his cantata *Arresta il passo* for performance at their Christmas party in July 1708, considerations of the weather forbidding their sitting in an arcadian grove during December. The stretched effort of these academicians to reach back into a world of charmingly imagined shepherds, nymphs and woodland spirits, their reordering of the calendar in the interests of a supper party, along with their fanciful adoption of bucolic names for their meetings, in no way suggests a serious contemplation of what the Greek myths might be saying about the enduring realities of heroism, loss, friendship, death and love. Handel must have been thoroughly unsatisfied by this sort of thing. The myths spoke more powerfully and more immediately in him.

He was now summoned, however, from Roman history and prettifying mythology to aristocratic romance. Whatever his pious father thought of such entertainments, Prince Ferdinando was not willing to abandon the Medici opera season. During Handel's years in Italy the Florentines put on operas by Alessandro Scarlatti, Giacomo Antonio Perti, Orlandini and Fago, and Handel knew at least enough of these productions to obtain copies of four of the librettos. He used texts that the Medici court poet, Antonio Salvi, had made for Perti operas in his own *Sosarme*, *Ariodante*, *Berenice* and *Rodelinda*. The Prince, in giving Handel a commission, expected something like the Hamburg *Almira*. But Handel now wanted to do things rather differently. He was coming to appreciate history as always faction and usually fiction. He was, for the rest of his career, to take incidents from the past and so shape their telling that audiences should perceive an emotional pattern in the action which touched their own lives. History, he was coming to understand, could be opened upon what he was also discovering to be declared in myth. His Hamburg employers had thought it a great thing that Keiser could bring recent Neapolitan riots onto the Gänsemarkt stage, and that, within three years of the Turk being at the gates of Vienna, Lucas von Bostel should show the Elector of Saxony spoiling for a fight with the pagans whilst an angel hovered protectingly overhead. Handel had no enthusiasm for this kind of relevance. In Florence he discerned rather more in the historical romance than was being explored in the unadventurous works of Perti.

The operas that Perti made for the Medici performances in their Pratolino villa placed events and characters at a further distance than mere time effects. These operas are diversions from reality. Indeed, Perti had only received the Pratolino commissions because Scarlatti had been dropped by Prince Ferdinando for constantly offering him music that was too demanding for his friends in the audience. Handel's 1707 *Rodrigo*, or, as the composer rather bulkily entitled the opera, *Vincer se stesso è la maggior Vittoria*, though produced 'under the protection of the Most Serene Prince of Tuscany', was not a Pratolino opera. *Rodrigo* was meant for the city, not the villa. Still, the piece deals with a complex of eighth-century aristocratic politics. Rodrigo is the king of Castille. His army has just defeated Evanco, king of Aragon. But the triumphant general returns to court to discover that the king has seduced his sister while he was fighting in his wars. Public and private passions intermingle with a nicely confusing effect until the seduced Florinda marries Evanco, and Rodrigo and his queen Esilena retire to a rustic hut, thus demonstrating the title's assertion that 'to conquer oneself is the more important victory'. The baby son of Rodrigo and Florinda is named heir to Castille.

Handel seized whatever opportunity the anonymous librettist gave him to emphasize everything that is humanly valuable in this story of power politics. Indeed, the climax of the opera at which the selfless Esilena, just when Florinda is grabbing a chance to kill Rodrigo, brings on the baby to kiss his father, is very much overemphasized. Aria upon aria presses home the lesson that magnanimity is better than revenge, however appalling the offence. But if the moral force of the situation is not competently presented to the Florentines, there can be no doubt that Handel intends his opera to have a moral force.

Handel had some success with *Rodrigo*. The Prince gave him a set of plate. Scarlatti, after the insufficiently diverting *Tamerlano* of 1706, had gone off to Venice and there proved himself an incorrigibly unpopular experimenter with *Mitridate Eupatore*. The two composers met up again in Rome during the spring of 1708 to prepare an ambitious Holy Week project. Ottoboni had a plan for Scarlatti's *Oratorio per la Passione*, for which the cardinal had written the text, to be put on in the Cancelleria for the Wednesday, and for Ruspoli to present Handel's *Oratorio per la Risurrettione di Nostro Signor Giesu Cristo* at the Palazzo Bonelli on Easter Day.

Thinking over the strangeness of the Lutheran amongst the Roman cardinals, Mainwaring asked 'How could these good Catholics be supposed to bear him any real regard, without endeavouring to lead him out of the road to damnation?' He has a story of a cardinal's attempt to get Handel into the Roman Church, and of the composer answering his persuasions with the modest affirmation that he was 'neither qualified nor disposed to enter enquiries of this sort, but was resolved to die a member of that communion, whether true or false, in which he was born and bred'. His continuing to live according to his Lutheran baptism certainly did not prevent Handel's entering into the devotional spirit of the Catholics around him. He realized that both words and music might cross over from community to community. He would as a boy have sung the great Pietist hymn 'O sacred head, sore wounded' that Paul Gerhardt (c. 1607–76) had derived from the Cistercian mysticism of 'Salve caput cruentatum'. Now, as a young man, he was making music for Marian petitions. His *Salve Regina* for Ruspoli has in our own time been described in terms of 'an unmistakable act of chivalrous devotion before the Queen of Heaven', of there being 'something mystic, dark and gripping about Handel's total commitment to this rapturous text'.[3] It seems very unlikely that, on hearing such a music, men as generous and sensitive as Ottoboni and Ruspoli would entertain thoughts of Handel's damnation. They were entirely content to share their celebration of the mystery of Easter with him. There is a dramatic intensity in the score of *La Resurrezione* (to use its modern name) which indicates that Handel is wholly caught up in the action of the oratorio. The occurrence of such dramatic intensity in his work is the only useful guide we now have to the composer's own beliefs.

Handel's music for *La Resurrezione* begins with a da capo aria in which an angel announces the Easter event to the cosmos. The first section of a da capo aria declares the musical theme and the range of expression determined for the aria. This is followed by a shorter second section, often in contrast to the material of the opening section. Once this counter-statement has been worked out, the aria returns to the musical structure of the first section, which is now repeated *da capo*, 'from the beginning'. An uninventive composer may settle for a straight second hearing of 'that strain again'. Handel could be lazy at times and offer just this plain repetition. More often, he understood that, like Orsino, his listener would, second time round, feel that the opening section was 'not so sweet now as it was before', and either he himself wrote a surprise into the repetition, or he prompted the singer to some musicianly decoration of the line. There were occasions when, exercising some theatrical cleverness, Handel would lull an audience into thinking that they were to hear a repeat and, tantalizingly, postpone the return of the first section, interrupt it, cut it short, or revise it into a new aria altogether. But, generally, in such a da capo aria, he was hoping to communicate the sense of being, at the end, 'at home' in a recognizable order. It was just such an order which he was announcing in *La Resurrezione*.

The opening aria places the hearer within the familiar world of scriptural quotation. The Angel's shout, 'Open up, you Gates of Hell', had been elaborated by Carlo Capece, another member of the Accademia Arcadiana, from the 'Petrine promise' of Matthew 16:18 and the 'King of Glory' verses of Psalm 24. Handel hesitated between several ways of making his Resurrection declaration. At one time he thought of beginning in unaccompanied speech and starting the music only when the Angel's order is disputed by Lucifero. Music would thus have been appreciable as the proper language of theological debate. Reconsidering this, he wondered if he should not start with a recitative and aria for Lucifero, as he triumphs in the death of Christ, and suddenly confront him with the awesome light of the resurrection angel. Finally, he wrote an overture leading straight into the Angel's aria, which was now thrillingly accompanied by the sound of trumpets from the other side. The Angel's trumpets rouse Lucifero from the dark recesses of hell. The music determines the action.

When he first comes from his darkness, Lucifero wholly misunderstands the situation. He calls to the 'Eumenidi' or Furies, those vengeful pursuers in the *Oresteia*, to rejoice with him at the killing of Jesus on the Cross. Like the demonic 'rulers of this age' in 1 Corinthians 2, they think that by crucifying the 'Lord of Glory' they have won a great victory. But in the debate with the Angel we hear the triumph of 'bel lume d'un lume' over the murkiness of 'Tartarea notte'.

The disciples at the tomb are even slower than Lucifero at catching on to what is happening in their world. They are less sensitive than he to the 'armonia gradita' of the angelic message. The Maddalena (Mary Magdalen), Cleofe and young Giovanni are figures of every Christian in Handel's audience. They begin in ignorance, even darkness, exercising a merely passive emotion in response to events. The Maddalena's 'Notte, notte, funesta' is a lament in the gloomy night for the ending of their hope at the Crucifixion. It is sung to the thin accompaniment of a few recorders. Her following aria, 'Ferma l'ali', with the recorders enhanced a little by muted violins, is perfectly expressive of her weary desire to keep faith with the dead: 'Fold your wings, do not brush across my eyes, ungrateful sleep'. Slowly, as Cleofe begins to look up, and Giovanni reminds the women of Christ's promise to rise again, Handel gives all his instruments a resurrection freedom. The sound rises magnificently. The climax of this part of the oratorio is a staggeringly well-organized piece of theologizing. The sleep of 'Ferma l'ali' gives way to a waking experience of the risen Lord. This is an experience which the librettist himself had admitted could not be expressed in words.

Durastanti's singing of 'Hò un non sò che nel cor' brought the wondering audience in Ruspoli's elegant salone to a realization that each one of them might joyfully confess 'I have I know not what within my heart'. Each of them is enabled to feel what the fullness of experience might be through the fullness of Handel's orchestral sound. His music gives an immediacy to that old Christian hymn preserved at Ephesians 5:14:

> Awake, O sleeper, and arise from the dead,
> And Christ shall give you light.

Capece's reminiscence of this hymn in his text, and of the angel's rescuing Peter from the dark prison at Acts 12:6–11, afforded Handel his first opportunity to express in his music that sense of liberation as a divine gift which was to be a permanent and important element in his maturest work.

The language of light's victory over the realm of darkness dominates the oratorio, not only through the reverberations of Capece's text, but, more feelingly yet, through the emphases of Handel's musical design. 'Behold the sun rising from the sea', sings the young Giovanni at the dawn of Easter Day, and in his 'Ecco il sol' we can hear Handel recapitalizing what he had learnt of the significance of Apollo whilst writing his Hamburg operas and Roman cantatas. We can hear, too, a recollection of the Pietist tradition of his schoolmasters. Handel is returning in Rome to the language of the Halle hymnists. For, together with the version that Johann Friedrich Starck (1680–1756) made of the Ephesians song:

> Arise from your graves, you dead;
> No more sleeping,
> You saints,

Handel's oratorio echoes Freylinghausen's more mythic verse:

> Now the sun in us does shine
> O uncreated sun
> Joy and happiness are mine
> Now this day's light's begun.[4]

At the close of the oratorio, the Maddalena's serenade to 'the beloved sun' opens into a chorus of 'a world awake', where, according to the patterns of the sun's passage from the horizon to high noon, those who are below are brought into heavenly heights. Her song bursts the confines of such palace entertainments. It is a sign of Handel's larger ambition. However pleasingly adventuresome his patrons found his cantata experiments, however much he was himself learning whilst making *Il Trionfo* and *Agrippina*, and however nearly the musical structures of *La Resurrezione* came to the condition of opera, he wanted to write for the public theatre. He could not do so in Rome.

The papal ban points to a difference in the expectations that Handel and his patrons had of opera. Innocent XI (Pope 1676–89) had not issued the original ban simply on account of a particularly scandalous incident at the carnival of 1677. The Pope had seen that opera in the Roman public theatres was an essentially trivial affair, a tickling of emotional responses which rendered frivolous the most serious situations. Love, honour, hatred, patriotism, despair became in opera merely the pretexts for extraordinary vocal displays. The Pope wished to prevent the relationships and emotions which gave dignity and purpose to human life from becoming mixed up with the leer of the stage-door Giovanni and the preening grimace of the castrati.

And back again

The 1708 *La Resurrezione* troubled the monsignori of the Curia rather more than its companion piece. They made no objection to the mid-week *Oratorio per la Passione*. Scarlatti's work could be plausibly retitled *Culpa, Poenitentia et Gratia* for later performances in Rome. It was no more operatic in design than *Il Trionfo del Tempo e del Disinganno*. But anyone who had gone to one of the three packed public rehearsals of *La Resurrezione* might have warned the censors that this was a dramatic work, purposeful in its delineation of distinct characters within a developing action. It was, as the Curial officials discerned for themselves at the first performance, opera in all but name. The monsignori knew that Clement XI (Pope 1700–21) had not appointed them so that they should permit the devaluation which had already occurred in operatic representations of the majesty of kings and the virtue of fair women to be extended to the dogmas of Christianity. It was as a counter to any such devaluating influence in society that the Pope that very year declared that the feast of the Immaculate Conception of Mary was to be kept throughout Christendom. They had to do something. So they insisted that Handel's splendid announcement of resurrection hope should not be made by a woman. The marchese was ordered to find a castrato to sing Maddalena at the Monday repetition of the oratorio.

Whilst the Curial officials may have been correct in their suspicion that the cardinals regarded the Scarlatti and Handel works as a pair of decent excuses for singing, scenery and supper, Handel certainly had other expectations of the performance. He meant to make a considered statement in his music, most especially in the music he had written for the great soprano, of just those values which the Pope had understood to be threatened in *opera seria*. Handel, after the Curial interference, began to think of working in some other city. And immediately after the success of the Easter oratorio, Handel was invited to Naples by another cardinal. The Viceroy, Vincenzo Grimani, was wholly unsympathetic to the Curial tone. He wanted an entertainment for a wedding at his court. Handel set to work on *Aci, Galatea e Polifemo* more with his own interests in mind than those of the bridal couple.

The story of Galatea, derived from Theocritus by way of Ovid, seems inappropriate to a wedding feast. But, then, opera begins with a performance at a Medici wedding of the equally inapposite tale of Eurydice. What did the myth of the nymph courted too roughly by the Cyclops Polyphemus, and too rashly by his handsome rival Acis, offer the composer? Once the young man has been changed into a stream, once the angry Cyclops has departed, and the nymph is left weeping on the shore, what did Handel hope his audience would remember from their story? It is evident that the librettist expected them to go home with a decent moral in mind. After the telling of the story, all three characters line up along the footlights, like the supporting cast at the close of *Don Giovanni*, to remind the audience that 'he who loves best has truth and constancy as his aim'. Handel's music for this finale does not undermine the moral, as the deliberately old-fashioned stuff of the postlude so evidently undermines the *Don Giovanni* message. But Handel's creative energy transforms the conventions of pastoral masque. He is not simply repeating what other composers had been doing for a hundred years. He presents Grimani's guests with emphatic characters in a dramatically significant action. It is to be noted, between the cakes and ices, that the 'truth and constancy' shown in this wedding serenata are attributes not of the romantic youth and nymph who have conducted their wooing behind a rock and who have run in opposite directions to save their skins when discovered, but of the rough, ugly Cyclops who has pursued his hopeless passion through the entire action. And Polifemo has the best music. Anyone who can manage the stretching range of 'Fra ombre e gli orrori' successfully is bound to be accorded huge applause. What did Handel intend by such a novel distribution of musical and dramatic weight? He was directing his hearers towards a more generous appreciation of what it is to be human. It is easy enough to fancy oneself a lovable boy or a pretty girl. Handel does not dismiss such identifications. But he does suggest that his hearers should identify also with the Cyclops. The Cyclops' fate is, after all, quite commonly their own.

Handel may have heard the 1702 *Polifemo* of Antonio Maria Bononcini (1677–1726), and he may, during his time in the Hamburg orchestra pit, have turned over the innovative French *Acis et Galatée* of 1689, but this entertainment perfectly expresses his own mind at this time. *Aci, Galatea e Polifemo* should be understood together with the many cantatas and serenatas he was composing at this time which are concerned with the impossibility of attaining one's desire, ambition, happiness. The couple at the Neapolitan marriage were being offered a music which fits with the Ruspoli cantatas of complaint against lovers who let their beloveds down. Sometimes these reach, as in 'Tu fedel, tu constante', a pitch of cynicism, but more usually they express the resignation of *Armida abbandonata*, or the luckless nobility of the Lucrezia *scena*, 'O numi eterni'. Only in *La Resurrezione* is human loss countered by an effective promise of freedom for those who sit in darkness and of reunion for those who have been parted. The final member of this sequence was an *Apollo e Dafne* in which the girl knows from the beginning that the bright god's wooing will bring disaster down on her.

Handel may have played his *Agrippina condotta a morire* to Grimani during his Neapolitan visit. And Grimani may have decided that Handel should be shown a different prospect of court life. At any rate, the cardinal wrote an *Agrippina* opera libretto for him, and arranged for it to be produced at the Teatro San Giovanni Grisostomo in Venice, which was owned by Grimani's relatives. The cardinal's cheerful text is replete with subtle digs at the varieties of Italian conspirator and eavesdropper as the plot moves along at a lively comic pace to the discomfort of any character who entertains a hope of outwitting the others. Handel proved as entirely capable of musical fun as of sorrow, but he arranged that it was the one man of good intentions among the characters who got the best tunes. Handel signals to his audience that Ottone is to be admired. His integrity sounds splendidly in a world ruled by the ambitious Agrippina, and his love is beautifully celebrated in the midst of a whirligig of passion set in motion by Poppaea. Handel indicates the moral hitching-posts in the hurly-burly of Grimani's cheerful satire. *Agrippina*, Mainwaring asserts, this time without fear of any contradiction from Mattheson, was performed 27 times successively in a city where two other opera houses were also presenting their seasons. But even whilst the Venetians were shouting their *viva il caro Sassone*, Handel was packing his bags.

He had evidently been thinking of returning to Germany even while he was in Florence, going to performances, looking over scores, collecting librettos, in November 1709. The Most Serene Ferdinando had then given him a letter of recommendation to Prince Karl von Neuberg, who was related to the Medici by Gian Gastone's unfortunate marriage to Princess Anna of Saxe-Lauenburg. The composer, however, proved on arrival to be a less than eager pensioner of the Innsbruck court. Prince Karl was soon reporting to Prince Ferdinando that Handel had continued his journey north, having 'no need of my assistance'.

Handel may have had assurances of a welcome in Hanover from Prince Ernst August, brother of the Elector of Hanover, who had been in Italy during the winter of 1707; he had certainly received an invitation from Baron Kielmansegge, the Elector's Master of Horse, in 1710, after the success of *Agrippina*. Immediately on his arrival, the Elector provided a court pension, following this very quickly with the offer of the post of Kapellmeister. It was just the sort of job his parents had wanted for him. Handel would be nicely niched in the Herrenhausen palace. His sense of 'his own bottom' was reconciled with his need for money when the Elector most generously agreed to Handel's going first to London for a year. He was anxious to hear what was going on in the English music halls. Leaving all legal matters to be dealt with by his *très honoré frère*, Michael Michaelsen, who had married his younger sister Dorothea in 1708, Handel set off.

Myth into opera: the first attempt

Between Hanover and London, Handel stopped off for a while at Düsseldorf. However distinguished the Elector Palatine Jan Wellems was, and however independently influential he thought his Palatinate, Düsseldorf was for Handel an outpost of the Medici connection. Prince Ferdinando's sister Anna Maria Louisa, who was to prove the most tenacious of the family, holding on to life, goods and disruptive influence years after the deaths of all her relatives, had married the Elector at Innsbruck in 1691. Perhaps she and her husband hoped to secure so Florentined a north German for their court, but the letters between the Electress and her brother show that she had to be content with Handel's choosing a 'northern' harpsichord for the Most Serene Prince. The Elector sent a courteous note acknowledging the sureness of Prince Ferdinando's judgement in recommending a virtuoso whose 'singular talents' had given the court great satisfaction during the several weeks of his stay in Düsseldorf.

Handel arrived in London late in November 1710, and found that

18

'Hò un non sò che nel cor', having, after its first appearance in the Rome *La Resurrezione*, been employed in the Venice *Agrippina*, was now being sung with new English words in Alessandro Scarlatti's *Pirro e Demetrio* at the Haymarket Theatre. The beauty of that aria had, Mainwaring was told, made many of the nobility 'impatient for an Opera of his composing'. Handel was equally impatient to get composing. He set to work on a text Italianized into *Rinaldo* by Giacomo Rossi. The librettist felt himself to have been rather too much hurried by the speedy mode of composing characteristic of 'the Orpheus of our century'. *Rinaldo*, 'the first he made in England, was finished in a fortnight's time'. It was also the first Italian opera that anyone had made especially for a theatre in England. Handel could be the speedier because he was plundering earlier works, especially the Roman cantatas, in the confidence that very few of his London patrons would have heard them. *Rinaldo* was a regathering of what Handel had achieved in Rome. And the London opera, since it also reuses material from *Almira*, represents a further retracing of his Hamburg steps which he had begun in *Agrippina*. He was now, after renewing the classical and romantic history elements of his Gänsemarkt enterprise, reconsidering the ways in which an opera might present myth.

He had been struggling since his last weeks in Italy with the difficulties of making a theatrical version of a myth. It would seem from the watermarks of the paper on which Handel wrote *Apollo e Dafne* that he began the cantata in Venice, continued writing on the journey through Lombardy, worked on it again in Germany, and finished it in London.[5] Whatever the interruptions, this dramatic cantata is superbly constructed. The action moves forward in the music with totally justified confidence. Apollo's opening announcement that 'the world is liberated' might seem to promise some further exploration of that relation of divine grace and the liberation of human beings begun in *La Resurrezione*, but these things are always more complex than we might suppose. In his claim that 'la terra e liberata' the god is making an unsustainable boast. Apollo, triumphing in his victory over the Python, declares his bow to be mightier than the puny weapon of little Cupid. Immediately, his rough complacence is shattered by the appearance of the lovely Dafne. Apollo is now love's prisoner. Dafne sings modestly, and most alluringly, of that 'Felicissima', that happy girl who is at peace because her heart is free. Their tragedy has already happened in the music. He is bound to attempt a conquest. She will run anywhere to escape his clutches. The moment when she is turned into the laurel is managed with as masterly an antithesis as the moment of their first meeting. The terrified girl is just about to be caught by the faster god when, at a sudden break in the music, Apollo finds himself grabbing at leaves. This is a powerful reworking of the myth. But its cantata form could not satisfy Handel's present ambition.

Meanwhile, *Rinaldo* was being produced. This opera has many of the elements of pantomime: a brave prince, a desolate heroine, a sorceress doing magic, a dragon breathing fire, transformation scenes and a ballet of agile spirits. But it is as much an exploration of mythic forces as an exploitation of theatrical machinery. The prince who sets out to rescue the kidnapped heroine from the sorceress describes his quest in terms of that great rescue myth which fascinated Handel all his working life. The prince identifies himself as Hercules. Winton Dean remarks that 'it is not clear why Rinaldo should threaten Cerberus, unless Handel took the aria from a lost cantata'.[6] If there were, indeed, an Italian cantata, an *Ercole*, it would be, with *La Resurrezione*, the earliest sign of Handel's celebrating the myth of the hero who brings the dead back to the living. But Handel's present use of this language, whether the music is recovered from a cantata or not, is a signal to his London audience of his mythic conception of what is going on in *Rinaldo*. Even so early in his operatic career, Greek myth is appreciated by Handel as having some kinship with Christian faith. After his combat with 'two Frightful Furies', Rinaldo rescues his lady from the infidel who so boastingly has sounded his 'Pagan Trumpets', and then effects the conversion of the sorceress. There is a splendid transformation scene when her magic mountains part to reveal the City of Jerusalem where all, pagan and Christian, may dwell in peace. All this is effected, perhaps, a trifle clumsily: Handel would learn how to do such things better. But the general scheme of the opera, working from Hercules in the Underworld to a community in Christ's Kingdom, seems perfectly clear.

The piece was much applauded, the effects as much as the singing. And in the midst of this hurrahing, as at the ball of another pantomime, the time arrived for Handel to return to Hanover.

He went back as slowly as he had come, stopping so long at Düsseldorf that Jan Wellems wrote notes on his behalf explaining the delay to both Elector George and his mother, the old Electress Sophia. Handel, however, thought only of getting back to London as soon as he decently could. He had a mythic opera in mind. As soon as the Elector went off on his annual September trip to the hunting lodge at Gohrde, Handel boarded the coach for England.

The 1712 season began badly for him. He wholly misjudged the way to insinuate anything like a mythic theme with London audiences. *Il Pastor Fido* was a colossal flop, even though Durastanti, who had come over to sing for him, repeated her rendering of 'Hò un non sò che nel cor' in the new piece. Handel had made a great mistake in suggesting that Nicola Haym (c. 1670–1729), who had been on the fringes of the Accademia Arcadiana, make him a version of Guarini's sixteenth-century diversion. It was an act of uncharacteristic timidity. *Il Pastor Fido* had been rightly judged by a number of composers as possessing enough energy for a madrigal or a shortish cantata, but not for an opera. The fiction of star-crossed lovers, mildly unsympathetic parents, and the restoration of a suddenly recognized heir, is too palely written to bear the sort of music Handel now wanted to make for a theatre audience. But, accepting its failure, Handel at once sat down to rescue his London reputation with *Teseo*.

Teseo was advertised as about to be presented with 'all ye Habits new, richer than ye former, with 4 New Scenes, other Decorations and Machines'. The expense of such baroqueries proved too much for Owen Swiney, the impresario; he fled to Italy, leaving composer, orchestra, carpenters and singers to carry on by themselves; which, to everyone's surprise, they did. In his first opera there had been a girl who loved a prince but who had suffered the unwanted addresses of his father. Handel's return in *Teseo* to the generation antagonisms of *Almira* should, since he was so much better equipped than at Hamburg, have allowed him now to develop a convincingly universal theme. But he could not yet find his way to harness the tragic energy in the father's recognition of his son's nobility and of the demand that such nobility properly makes upon a generous authority. There is nothing in *Teseo* to rival Mozart's attempts at the same theme of generation gaps in *Idomeneo* and *Die Zauberflöte*. And the extravagant machinery of the production had the effect of disturbing the dramatic balance of the opera.

Swiney had arranged to bring a *dea* down in a *machina* to make all click into the happy ending, *lieto fine*, demanded in *opera seria*. Handel's conviction that it is not by such epiphanies but by human mediations that the divine is revealed to us is heard in Minerva's blessing being sung by her human priest. At the same time, again by purely musical means, Handel makes his audience aware of the peculiarity of divine graciousness in our world. The priest is the solitary bass amidst a cast of sopranos and altos. The finale of *Teseo* was intended by the composer to suggest that the divine order is discernible in the arrangements of their lives that the hero and the old king have made together. Minerva, through her priest, declares that their human understanding is in accord with her will. But the splendour of the new and richer costumes and of the new machine in which she descends suggests a different interpretation of what is going on. Minerva seems a miraculous intrusion into human mistakings: her blessing seems to reveal an order that is wholly transcendent. Handel would have to do rather more to persuade the British that opera plots of nymphs and heroes and goddesses had a reference to the life they experienced beyond the theatre box and gallery.

It was now time for him to return to Germany, but, says Mainwaring, whether because he was afraid of being seasick again on the Channel crossing, or whether he had taken a liking to British cooking, his promise to return 'had somehow slipt out of his memory'. The performances of the *Birthday Ode* in February 1713, and the rehearsals in March of the *Te Deum* and *Jubilate* to celebrate the Treaty of Utrecht, showed him to be a very British composer. Queen Anne's surviving yet another year cannot have given much pleasure to the court of her designated heir the Elector of Hanover, who had publicly denounced the terms of the Treaty.

Within a month of the July thanksgiving service in St Paul's, Queen Anne had died and a squadron had been sent to Holland to escort the Elector into his kingdom. George I had, not unnaturally, thought it inappropriate that a man who had so settled into London life and who was enjoying a pension from the Stuart court should continue to receive a stipend from Hanover as an absentee Kapellmeister. Handel seems to have been unnaturally surprised when his pay was stopped in June 1713. But the dismissal was conveyed to him by Baron Kielmansegge with the accompanying assurance that 'he is by no means in disgrace' and that 'when some day His Highness comes here, he might re-enter his service'. So it proved. It remains true, however, that the early years of the reign were not good for the composer. His new opera *Amadigi di Gaula* was not a success in 1715, and the season was cut short by the scare of the Jacobite invasion early in the summer. The next season began very late and not much money was made by anyone in the theatre. So when George I went over to Hanover in July 1716, Handel was content to follow him.

On this visit, probably, Handel composed his setting of a Passion text by Barthold Hinrich Brockes (1680–1747). The *Brockes Passion* recoups something of what Handel is likely to have known not only from the Roman settings of Scarlatti but also from the Lutheran *historie* of his Halle childhood. Whilst the mediaeval singing of the Passion had been developed as a way of announcing the text of a gospel, the *historie* was usually a setting of some redaction of the four gospels so that what was taken to be their shared meaning could be concentratedly declared to the congregation. The scriptural text was persuaded to render up its relevance to contemporary German lives. Whatever the circumstantial differences of time, place and experience between author and audience, the mediating composer was to declare the immediacy of evangelical meaning. Handel recognized the likeness of the *historie* version of the gospels to what he had been feeling his way towards in his considerations of myth.

The *Brockes Passion* is a *historie* in vernacular verse, but it is also a practice space for that translation from cantata to opera, and from doctrine to myth, which Handel had begun in *La Resurrezione* and was continuing through *Aci, Galatea e Polifemo* into *Teseo*. Handel's setting gives a much greater prominence than was usual in the *historie* both to individual persons of the story, Mary and Judas and, most especially, Jesus, and to meditations on events by a series of onlookers with whom the congregation is to identify: 'the Daughter of Zion', 'Believing Souls' and 'the Christian Church'. We may now discern in all this the beginnings of the dramatic oratorio, but in 1716 Handel was not planning a career as an oratorio-maker. The likeness that was then most evident to the composer was a likeness to opera. That admiring exploration of the demand made by the nobility of a son on the graciousness of a father which had escaped him in *Teseo* is clearly a driving force in the construction of the Passion. The climactic moment of his music is in Jesus' prayer on the Mount of Olives: 'Mein Vater! Schau, wie ich mich quale'.

Though the *Brockes Passion* had a little local success, and Handel was gratified to know that he had done well with a text already set by his old Hamburg colleagues, including Mattheson, he was not now going to settle for less than the Londoners' applause at a variety of story-tellings. He returned to England late in 1716. And there, his concern for narrative as a communication of meaning, his feeling for the Christian reference of myth and for the remythologization of Christian teaching made him a central, if unprofessional, figure for the eighteenth-century debates initiated by the deist writers.

Notes

1   For Keiser and Hamburg opera generally, see W. Dean and J. M. Knapp, *Handel's Operas 1704-1726* (1987), pp. 38–77.

2   Cf. J. S. Hall, 'Handel among the Carmelites', *Dublin Review* 233 (1959), p. 121.

3   Cf. P. M. Young, *Handel* (1946); and H. C. Robbins Landon, *Handel and his World* (1984), p. 51.

4   Cf. J. F. Starck, *Tägliches Handbuch* (Constance, n.d.), Part IV; and
    J. A. Freylinghausen, *Geistreiches Gesangbuch* (Halle, 1705), no. 615.

5   Cf. Landon, *op. cit.*, p. 74 and endnote.

6   Dean and Knapp, *op. cit.*, p. 178.

2

Deist debates in Britain

FROM STILLINGFLEET'S *ORIGINES SACRAE* (1662) TO *ADMETO* (1727)

The conduct of the deist debates, however complex the contro-versialists' accounts of their philosophical instruments (of analogical predication, for example), and however subtle their management of theological distinctions, particularly in defining their doctrines of the Trinity, may be quite simply characterized: those who came to be labelled unorthodox were cheerfully pointing to similarities between the stories preserved in the Bible and those of other cultures, to which those who established themselves as representative of ortho-doxy responded by dissociating Christian teaching from every sort of story-telling. The significance of these debates for the culture of eighteenth-century England lay in their powerful suggestion that it was not appropriate for sensitive and intelligent women and men to speak of their experience in any narrative form, biblical or not.

In later stages of this controversy the participants had an eye to the newly discovered religions of Africa and America, but their first ques-tions arose from reconsiderations of the established story-tellings of the Greeks and the Romans and their relation to the biblical stories of Israel. The history of this reconsideration in Britain is enticingly complex, but its general direction may be traced as a series of respon-ses to the kind of thing exhibited in Edward Stillingfleet's *Origines Sacrae* of 1662,[1] a book designed first to identify in the Bible those historical facts from which the fictions of foreign religions have deviated, and then to encourage, after an enlightened abandonment of every other myth and story, the retention of that biblical history as a guide to the world as it has been and still is.

'The origin of the Heathen mythology'

Stillingfleet's investigations start from the belief that, since all mankind is the posterity of Noah, it is to be expected that a witness to the God who preserved Noah would be discernible in the traditions of all nations, not the Hebrews only, although by degrees it would be so much altered 'for want of certain records to preserve it in' that we would now be unable to discover the original 'without an exact comparing it with the true history itself'. Stillingfleet expects, that is, to discover among the heathen legends some distorted version of the books of Moses. He has a nice folk-tale simile for his way of detecting the original within the version:

> It fared with this tradition of the first ages of the world, as with a person who hath a long time travelled in foreign parts, who by the variety of the climes and countries, may be so far altered from what he was, that his own relations may not know him upon his return, but only by some certain marks which he hath upon his body.

Stillingfleet's scholarly enterprise is concerned to establish, from the strawberry markings on the lost boy, those 'remainders of the Scripture-history' in heathen mythology, the process by which the historical narratives of the Hebrews were corrupted. He begins with an exploration of what the heathen have remembered of Noah's account of the first human beings.

It is an easy business to discern in the 'Phoenician theology' fragmentary references to the chaos of Genesis, the evening which followed it, the creation of angels, and the making of Adam from the earth. Stillingfleet comes, with some help from the researches of the great German Calvinist classical scholar Vossius (1577–1649) into the meaning of Tacitus, to that same making of Adam in the stories of the German tribes. He then engages in a charmingly erudite hunt to make out what happened to Adam amongst more civilized peoples. In Cilicia there is a city called Adana, which is 'thought to have some remainder of the name of Adam'. The Greeks pronounced 'Adam' as 'Adan', and 'Adanus' is said by Stephanus de Urbibus, the Byzantine commentator on Homer, to be 'the son of Heaven and Earth' and thus 'Saturn himself'. Stillingfleet is especially happy to remark that 'Adam's hiding himself from the presence of the Lord gave the occasion to the name of Saturn, from *satar*, to hide', and that 'that power which Saturn had, and was deposed from, doth fitly set out the dominion man had in the golden age of innocency, which he lost by his own folly'. Stillingfleet goes on to review Adam's immediate family, finding 'something of Cain' preserved in Phoenician antiquities, of his wife in the Roman Vesta, of Tubalcain in Vulcan from 'the very great affinity' of both their names and their occupations, and of Jubal in Apollo, and, he says, Naamah may 'come in for' Minerva. This last phrase must have made Stillingfleet pause in some consciousness of the constructive character of his enterprise. He concludes at once. 'Thus we see there were some, though but obscure, footsteps preserved even of that part of Scripture-history which preceded the flood.' The Hebrew patriarchs being disguised by language and disfigured by legend, those who inherit the Jewish tradition in the Christian Churches may very well, like the relations of that traveller returned from foreign parts, take a little time to recognize them when they come back as Greek and Roman gods.

The corruption has increased at every telling of the tradition. This is, for Stillingfleet, a function of the linguistic confusion persisting after Babel. The Greeks, for example, having received the history of the race in the Hebrew language, translated the texts rather insensitively, paying insufficient attention to 'the idiom of the tongue'. Noah's being a 'husbandman' led to Saturn being the 'husband' of Rhea. The Hebrew for parturition being 'to come out of the thigh' led to Bacchus being born of Jupiter's thigh. And the Greeks elaborated what they did not understand. Gradually, 'the fabulousness of the poets' so disguised the Hebrew history that the truth of events and persons could not be recovered by simple folk. The educated investigator can, however, discern the original forms.

Stillingfleet is determinedly literary in his account of religion. He does not care for those who look for evidences of an historical basis for events, persons and places in the pagan stories. He will have nothing to do with those who potter among 'spurious Etruscan antiquities'. He concentrates the reader's attention on those offending poets. Not content with producing elaborated versions of events which they knew to have happened not to their own people but to the Hebrews, they had invented a past where they could not borrow one. Leaving behind its origin in history, the mythical account of the world developed into the fictional. The poets turned language against itself. 'They omitted that sense which was plain and obvious, and took that which was more strange and fabulous.' The Golden Fleece story, for example, was developed from the ambiguity of one Syriac word which could mean both 'fleece' and 'treasury', and helped along a little by another word's ambiguity as it hovered between 'brass' and 'dragon'. Stillingfleet is ever urging his reader to appreciate 'how easy a matter it was' for these word-mongering poets 'to advance the Heathen mythology from the equivocation of the Oriental languages, in which their traditions were conveyed to them'.

Once the linguistic argument has been established, it becomes apparent that the priests of the heathen, who saw in the poets' work an advantage for themselves, have gone on elaborating the stories of the particular divinities in whose service they achieved respect and fortune. These clerics did not require much from the Hebrew history in order to make a narrative for themselves. Stillingfleet liked to show that what was recorded of a single human being in the Scriptures was large enough to be the original of several gods. He trumped the suggestion of the Frenchman Samuel Bochart (1599–1667), whose two-volume *Geographica Sacra* (1641, 1646) and *Hierozoicon* (1663) were full of such etymological delights, that there were at least fourteen parallels between Saturn and Noah. 'Not only under Saturn, but under Prometheus too, was Noah's memory preserved.' Again, Janus, facing both ways, is obviously Noah seeing the ages before and after the Flood. Then, again, Bacchus was derived from the wine-loving Noah. 'Withal, Philostratus, in the Life of Apollonius, relates that the ancient Indian Bacchus came thither out of Assyria.' This 'yet more fully agrees' with all that we know about Noah. At the close of similar reviews of the pagan mythologies associated with Abraham, Isaac and Jacob, and the hero Moses, Stillingfleet feels it to be quite safe to remark that 'from this wonderful agreement of Heathen mythology with the Scriptures, it cannot but appear that the one is the corruption of the other'.

Once comparisons have been made, however, it may be difficult to halt them. The effect of such early attempts at understanding other folk's religion was to set the scriptural narratives in parallel with untrusted ways of story-telling. If the myths of other folk are corruptions of the Hebrew record, may not that record itself be a corruption of some even older history? To this question, John Julius Toland (1670–1722) addressed himself with some cheerfulness.

The origins of Christian mystery

Toland was, it was said by those who liked neither Toland nor Rome, the illegitimate son of an Irish priest. He became a convert to Protestantism in middle youth, studied at Leyden and Oxford at the cost of his new coreligionists and, as Sir Leslie Stephen remarked, 'repaid their generosity by acquiring a considerable amount of learning and then by suddenly firing *Christianity not Mysterious* in their faces'. That was in 1696. The book was immediately notorious. Toland fled back to Ireland, but partly, as Stephen suggests, because Toland talked in coffee houses and public drinking places instead of keeping his opinions for aristocratic supper parties, he was thought as much a nuisance in Dublin as in Middlesex. Robert South (1643–1716), a High Church prosecutor of a series of dubiously orthodox divines, was delighted to report that the Irish parliament 'sent him packing, and, without the help of a faggot, soon made the kingdom too hot to hold him'.[2]

Toland, not caring for those who clambered into power on the accession of Queen Anne in February 1702, took himself off to Hanover, where Leibniz (1646–1716), the tame historian of the Elector's family, who was always interested in *un homme d'esprit et de savoir*, noted that the court generally was not pleased to entertain so compromising a guest. The Electress Sophia herself, however, after some diplomatic pretences, 'received Toland with unfeigned pleasure'.[3] She was very soon made to realize that she was doing her claim to the succession no good in England, and by November she had given up his conversation. Toland had no better fortune in Berlin, and though he was received by the Elector Palatine in Düsseldorf, he was forced to make a hasty departure after 'an incident too ludicrous to be mentioned' by his biographer.[4] When he returned to Hanover in the summer of 1707, the old Electress could not resist taking him back into favour. The English minister protested. Her German ministers passed on the protest.

On neither of his visits to Hanover could Toland have talked deistry with Handel. In the spring of 1702 the composer had been playing the organ in the cathedral loft at Halle, and in 1707 he was with the cardinals in Rome. But it is likely that when Handel was himself in Düsseldorf and the conversation turned to London and its citizens that Toland would have been the subject of some lively reminiscence by the Elector Palatine and his Medici wife. Toland had written a nice little defence of the Elector's policy of persecuting Protestants in his land. Again, in Hanover, the theologically excitable Leibniz might have mentioned the dangerous innovator to the composer. Toland, like Handel, lost financially by the bursting of the South Sea Bubble. He died a poor pensioner of Lord Molesworth, who had promised 'to secure him the necessaries of life'. Handel had very early on discovered the unreliability of such aristocrats. He was never anyone's pensioner.

Toland's book was the famous occasion of a hard-hitting debate between Stillingfleet, now Bishop of Worcester, and the great John Locke (1632–1704), whom he rather fumblingly accused of deistical leanings. 'The Bishop's instincts were better than his reasoning powers', Stephen observed.[5] Locke's Christology does have a great deal in common with a deistical assessment of Jesus as simply the messenger who announced the existence of God and the duty of Man. But what Stillingfleet wrote against *Christianity not Mysterious* was so wide of the argument that 'Mr Toland does not know his own Book in the Bishop's Representation of it'.[6] Perhaps Stillingfleet deliberately misread the book, for it contained much that he must have recognized as being generally established during the discussions provoked by the French Oratorian Richard Simon (1638–1712) in his *Nouvelles observations sur le texte et les versions de Nouveau Testament* (1695), and the Arminian biblical scholar Jean LeClerc in his *Ars Critica* (1696). Toland himself would publish a translation of LeClerc's 'De l'incredulité' article for the *Bibliothèque universelle et historique* (1697).

Toland begins *Christianity not Mysterious* by brightly remarking how odd it is that men should make most noise in praise of what they profess least of all to understand: 'It may easily be concluded I mean the Mysteries of the Christian religion'. More: Christians seem to disagree most noisily about the ways in which they cannot understand their own Mysteries. They make divers unreasonable appeals for their modes of incomprehension. Anglicans refer to the judgement of the 'Fathers' or the 'Councils', Roman Catholics to 'those chimerical supreme Headships and Monsters of Infallibility' with which they have adorned their leaders. Toland is equally quick to accuse Protestants of being obfuscate in their appeal to 'the Scriptures'. By 'the Scriptures' they always mean the Scriptures conformed to their 'bulky System and Formularies' out of Switzerland or Scotland. Toland himself only means to prove, as the subtitle cf his book declares, that 'there is nothing in the Gospel contrary to Reason'.[7] No Christian is actually maintaining that Reason and Gospel are contraries, but very many will allow that 'according to our conceptions of them' and 'by reason of our corrupt and limited understanding', they may well seem to clash. The famous patristic suggestion that we should adore what we cannot comprehend, Toland believes to be 'the undoubted source of all the absurdities that were ever seriously vented among Christians'.

This reference to the absurdities of Christianity indicates what is new in Toland's account of the past. Stillingfleet had been careful to speak differently of Christianity from all other representatives of the primitive revelation. He talked of the curiosities of other religions without pausing to look in Christianity for the odd sign of a corruption of original manners. Toland changes all that. He looks as closely at biblical revelation as at mythologies.

Toland begins his study of Christianity, as Stillingfleet had begun his study of heathendom, with a consideration of what the religious language reveals. He suggests that our ordinary acquaintance with the variableness of the way 'the country people' speak in Scotland from the 'correct' English of the capital should be a guide in approaching the Hebrew of the Old Testament and the Greek of the New. He is much before his time in distinguishing the *koinē*, the 'common' dialect of the Hellenistic world in which the New Testament is written, from the language of Athenian literature. He would have the exegete seek the sense of a word from its uses, encouraging comparison not only of the Old Testament with the New and the New with the Old, but of both with the continuing Hebrew tradition of the Talmud which, 'however otherwise useless', allows 'no small light into the ancient rites and languages' of the biblical culture. Toland is an early employer of an historical method.

It is an historical method which, as the allegation of 'country' and 'correct' usage illustrates, is controlled by a belief that essentially things have always been as they are now. The control does work well in the *koinē* instance. It is not necessarily so helpful when it enables Toland to rule out both Old and New Testament miracle stories as being too unlike anything we experience now. Toland talked of 'the true Characters of Historical Evidence' and he assumed that everyone would both understand what he meant and agree with him. By a proper use of the divine gift of natural reason everyone has always been and will always be able to discern whether a story is history. Toland's assumptions did not allow him to consider any suggestion that Christianity itself might not be wholly in accord with 'our ordinary Ideas' of what is going on, or that a story-telling which affronted such ideas could be anything but a deception, unworthy of the God in whose name it was spread abroad. He did not trouble himself with such foolish speculations. 'Why should good Reasons be spent in the confutation of mere Fictions?' All human beings will, if they read with 'that equity and attention that is due to mere humane works', come to discover what is actually being communicated through the Scriptures. He anticipates *Essays and Reviews* (1860). 'Nor is there any different rule to be followed in the interpretation of Scripture from what is common to all other books.'

Since the evangelists 'were employed to dispel Ignorance, to eradicate Superstition, to propagate Trust and Reformation of Manners', readers should, unless their reason is distorted by some accidental indisposition of their organs, or they have brought on a defeat of their reasoning powers by some vicious habit, be sensitive to the consonance of Scripture with Reason. And if the official version of what is being proposed in these narratives does not appear reasonable to reasonable folk, it must be because, 'more or less in every place', human beings have succumbed to the charms of rituals dangled before them by priesthoods. Toland lumps together 'the Papists' and 'the Jews' and 'the Mahometans' with all those American Indians and African Negroes whose credulity 'makes them a Merchandize to their Priests'.

Priests have always and everywhere supposed that 'the common people will sooner believe what is unintelligible, incomprehensible, and above their Reasons, than what is easy, plain, and suited to their Capacities'. Toland observed that 'the vulgar are more oblig'd to Christ', for he thought them fit for straightforward instruction. He preached to them in good set terms, 'and they heard him gladly'. Toland took the parables of Jesus to be concerned with the quiet decencies of life, with practical co-operation and lawful obedience. There was no mystery about any of this. No sign of anything beyond 'our ordinary Ideas'. And once the code of conduct advocated in the stories had been identified, the Christian may abandon the stories and get on with the conduct. 'Everyone knows how the primitive Christians in imitation of the Jews turned all the Scriptures into Allegories.' Toland wanted nothing to do with anything of that sort: 'Type, Symbol, Parable, Shadow, Figure, Sign, and Mystery, signify all the same thing'.

Toland's examples of 'Mystery' and mystery story were almost all taken from the religions of the classical world. They told of Demeter and Eleusis, Bacchus and the Roman Carnival. But in this he was already rather old-fashioned. Others were talking more of the American Indian and the African Negro and the divers people of India. In the theatre, Dryden had shown twenty years before that *Aureng-Zebe* (1675) could speak in as heroic a verse as the romantic *Almanzor and Almahide* (1670, 1671) or the Roman Antony of *All for Love* (1677). This extension of the range of a gentleman's reference had made a difference in the conduct of the argument about Scripture. Toland himself began to read about 'the customs of the East Indians'.

Europeans and others

There were a number of travelling men telling tales in the late seventeenth century which set Western European beliefs and practices in open comparison with the doings of strange tribesmen. Richard Blome, describing the *Present State of His Majestie's Isles and Territories in America* (1687), assumed that his talk of Indian 'priests and conjurers' in New England would set his readers meditating on the likelihood of all priests being conjurers. He pressed the likeness of priesthoods by pointing out that the American priests of New York told their congregations that 'their god will accept no offering but money' which the priests take up, 'putting it into some dishes' on their altars.[8] From this similarity of practice it would be, Blome supposed, a short step to his readers' making some comparison with the Christian doctrine. They would put their Christian beliefs in judgement with the savages' talk of their devil. Blome encouraged them to take some careful note of the Sagamore who entertained many 'whimsical notions' about a trinity of 'one Son, one Mother, and the Sun'. What is appreciated as grasping or foolish in the American context cannot be seriously maintained in Christendom. Even the Indian could produce an ironic comment on the peculiar doctrine of the Christians: 'Being questioned if they or their Ancestors had heard that God was come into the World', the Sagamore of Newfoundland said 'he had not seen him'.

A more dangerous undermining of Christian doctrine was worked in William Bosman's *New and Accurate Description of the Coast of Guinea*, published in 1704 and already translated into English by 1705. The world had grown larger, and the Negro had been interrogated as well as the Indian. Bosman, who was the Dutch factor at the fort of Elmira, makes a similarly linking reference to savage and European priesthoods. He observed that before some great design, animal offerings were made 'by which the priest is sure to be the greatest gainer', for the god is to eat only the entrails of the sacrificial animal, and the people are to pay the priest for making the sacrifice on their behalf. Bosman, like Toland, connects rapacious priesthood with elaborate ritualizing. 'If it were possible to convert the Negroes to the Christian religion, the Roman Catholicks would succeed better than we should' because the savages were already used to priests who demanded that they observe strange fasts on the authority of a tradition which only the priests could interpret.[9]

If the maintainers of Protestant orthodoxy were content with these collatings of the Catholic and the savage, no Christian could remain unperturbed at other aspects of Bosman's work. He was impatient with any attempt to explain the character of native religion in parallel with Stillingfleet's explanation of Greek and Roman cults. He would not allow that the belief of the Gold Coast natives that 'the first men came out of Holes' in the ground, that they had to make an immediate choice between power and knowledge and had their sexual organs 'placed more in view' than at present, evidenced their tales as corruptions of some original awareness of Hebrew history. Nor, more significantly, would he allow that the religions of the natives he met should be interpreted as decadence from a primitive devotion to the one God revealed in nature. Whatever the savages knew of naked men coming from the earth, they knew nothing of one God who created all that is. The Africans had first heard of such a God when the European missionaries arrived and 'endeavoured to plant this Notion in them'. Contrariwise, the savages assured him that from their very beginning time they had known many gods. Bosman, too, has his dig at the Roman Catholics. He remarks that the clever Italians had not yet hit on a way of getting rid of an enemy that was 'so distinguishing and discrete' as the poison controlled by each particular patron spirit which, at the savage's prayer, would kill only the designated enemy however many others eat from the pot.

Neither Deist nor Protestant nor Catholic among these early dippers into anthropological studies could allow what Bosman was saying about the Gold Coasters to be taken as a paradigm of what was happening in religions generally. There was a demand for the assembling of evidence for primitive monotheism. Toland understood that the great problem for the historian was to identify 'by what means the Reason of men became so deprav'd, as to think of subordinate Deitys'.[10] He favours an explanation that begins in human beings' observation that all things are fragile, subject to decay, mortal. Wanting to pretend to themselves that some of their race have not been subject to dissolution, they have placed heroes in heaven: 'All superstitions originally related to the Worship of the Dead'. He made his contribution to the defence of primitive monotheism by translating de la Créquinière's clutch of foreign evidences as *Agreement of the Customs of the East Indians with those of the Jews* in 1705. There was a nicely double-edged significance for Toland in de la Créquinière's admission that 'while the ancient authors have given me support for several happy conjectures concerning the savages, the customs of the savages themselves have thrown much more light on the ancient authors'.[11]

But, for a while, the British were distracted from considerations of the travellers' tales of exotic natives in the excitement of attending to a novel form of European entertainment and rehearsing again a well-known and well-loved set of theological arguments.

On 16 January 1705, Christopher Rich opened his Drury Lane theatre with the suitably foreign *Arsinoe, Queen of Cyprus* by Thomas Clayton. The piece, though sung in English, was designed by impresario and composer to 'introduce the *Italian* manner of Musick on the English Stage'. Poor Vanbrugh, who had greater claim to be knowledgeable and enthusiastic about opera than his rival, was pipped at the post. Only on 9 April could he present Jakob Greber's *Gli amori d'Ergasto* at the Haymarket. His opera was sung in Italian. The audience did not care for such unintelligibility; the experiment failed. Rich was the cleverer impresario, and managed things more gradually. In March 1706 he produced a translated version of a 1697 *Il trionfo di Camilla* by Giovanni Bononcini, which he promised would give his audiences an authentic 'Taste of the *Italian* Musick'.

This tasting pleased. The British were ready to see and hear for themselves the truth of even stranger stories brought back by travellers who had spent an evening of their Grand Tour at an Italian opera house. By December 1706 the first castrato, Valentino Urbani, had arrived to sing in the next year's spring programme. Things were gradually becoming more Italian in the London theatre. Urbani, adopted by audiences as 'Valentini', was all the rage. In February 1708 he starred in his own adaptation of *Il trionfo d'amore*, one of Cardinal Ottoboni's little entertainments, and was the more wildly applauded. It could not be long before an opera to an Italian text would be especially composed for the English theatre.

In the midst of these rather louche delights, the British had been settling comfortably to listen to the reassuringly traditional abuse of a controversy brought back into polite conversation by the Boyle lecturer of 1704 and 1705. Samuel Clarke (1675–1729) had offered *A Demonstration of the Being and Attributes of God* which should bring natural and revealed religion into decent harmony. Clarke had intended to say something relevant to the deist debates, but within his sermons lurked speculations which disturbed Leibniz in Hanover and, in their more elaborate expression in Clarke's *Scripture-Doctrine of the Trinity*, occasioned even English accusations of 'Arianism'. Such accusations, with the counter-accusations of 'Sabellianism', afforded great satisfaction to professional disputers; name-calling of this sort gave rise then, as it usually does, to a progressive controversy that moves from talk of how the Son is 'like' and how 'unlike' the Father, through attempts at defining 'like' and 'unlike', to end in talk about how we are 'alike' and how it is that others are 'unlike' our orthodox selves. But, in this instance, the answerers came round again to considerations of what the biblical narratives were 'like'. Britishers were again occupied with this question. Even 'Arianism', even, it was to prove, 'Predestination', could not keep them away from considerations of biblical story-telling for any length of time. This re-arrangement of the discussion is demonstrated in the contribution of the Archbishop of Dublin, William King (1650–1729), who the orthodox thought had nicely settled the intermediary question about the language of 'like'.

From narrative to analogy

In that leisure which the state of religion in Ireland imposed upon the episcopate of the established Church in the eighteenth century, King had set himself to identify the ways in which it was still possible to maintain the language of the scriptural witness to God. His consideration of the biblical narratives was conducted under the flag of an enquiry into *Divine Predestination and Foreknowledge*. In 1709, the year before Handel first visited London, King published a pamphlet version of a sermon he had recently preached on this topic on his recovery from a particularly severe attack of gout. Discussion of predestination is likely to coincide with discussion of narrative, for both have to concern themselves with an authorial management of events which proceed in a temporal sequence within which their author does not belong, and which have the appearance of proceeding without management. But King, in order to stay with predestination, attempts to abandon narrative.

He appreciates that the predestination terminology he is using cannot be found, at least in its academic form, in the biblical stories. He thinks that he can deal with this gap in language by a quick reference to literary genres.

There is something resistant to the instruments of an exact science, such as theology, in a literary work designed to persuade, such as the Bible. King means to translate the topic from biblical anthropomorphisms to theological definitions: from 'comparison' and 'resemblance' and 'type' and 'parabolic figure' to 'analogy'. He concentrates attention on the inadequacy of the literary devices for serious work. And he has a modern instance ready to please those travellers who have lately come to figure in theologians' conversation. When he looked at a map of China it was not to make some helpful analogy of the map being to the country as revelation is to the Lord, but to show how foolish it would be for a person, from the 'similitude' or 'resemblance', to take China to be no bigger than the map which represents it. So with the Scriptures. They offer 'faint shadows' or 'emblems' or 'resemblances' of what exists in God, and a sensible man cannot rest content with such things. King would put a stop to that undisciplined talk of God's dealings with the human race which had been continuing in British commentaries upon Scripture since the first copies of Alciati's *Emblemata* arrived in the kingdom in 1593. From that book all those distracting notions of some prefiguring of Christ in myths of Apollo and Hercules and the rest arose. But King found himself unable to cut a way to a straightforward vocabulary of predestination. He had himself to resort, if not quite to 'type' and 'emblem', then certainly to 'parabolic figure'.

King would suffer the reasonable theologian to speak of the 'Wisdom', 'Understanding' and 'Foreknowledge' of God, but of very little else. Our reason teaches us to ascribe these attributes to God by way of 'analogy' to 'powers or qualities as we find them most valuable and perfect in ourselves'. But when he offers an example of this analogy of perfection, King presents an exercise of irrational power. 'I can', he observes, 'no more expect to escape free when I break the Laws and Rules he has prescribed me, than a subject can who assaults his Prince in the midst of all his guards', though the Prince may, among many condemned men, choose to 'reprieve one for an instance of his Mercy and Power and suffer the rest to be carried to Execution'. A pardoned sinner is such a reprieved felon. God is the arbitrary Prince. Such an impression of the divine cannot have been quite what King intended. Analogy has been subverted by narrative.

King has come very near to making a serviceable parable for one form of predestination thesis. His story has the surprise of the New Testament examples of parable; and it leaves the destination of women and men wholly within the decision of God. But he could not care for his own story. Putting it aside, he dissociates New Testament doctrine from every narrative form.

He continues to develop the distinction of theological science from biblical story-telling as a distinction of knowing from doing. The parables of Jesus are receivable, even by those who have no theological knowledge, as instructions for practical living. In some way which King does not even begin to elucidate, the repetition of the story, whether to learned divine or ignorant peasant, makes a demand on the hearer to behave in a godly manner. The parables 'oblige us to perform the Duties he requires at our hands'. So the theologian, as he proceeds from narrative to analogy, may leave 'plain honest people' in their 'figurative knowledge', confident that they are persuaded by parable to 'the substantial and real Duties of Religion'.[12]

King supposed that if the Christian were to 'prosecute the Methods prescribed in Scripture', a decent discernment of spirits would be his reward. As Bishop of Derry, he had been chief among those who made Ireland too hot for Toland in 1697. But he had never been much worried about ordinary Episcopalian Britishers being susceptible to deistical argument. When Lord Molesworth approached him in search of a job for Toland long afterwards, the Archbishop remarked on the difficulty of placing such a client, for 'the notion of religion' being so much a part of men's habitual outlook, 'the Generality never have esteem for one they believe has none'. Such a one will be 'detested and abhorred'.[13] King was sure, also, like the greater part of the superior Anglican clergy, that the 'Generality' would remain obediently unconvinced by the new talk of traders and travellers about stories and the Bible, even if their pastors and theologians failed to provide an account of how biblical story-telling generated an obligation.

If the telling of stories prompted, indeed commanded, action in the world as God has made it by women and men as God has made them, a good theologian should be concerned with the undefined character of stories at least as intently as with the categories of analogical predication. But King pushed on to examine the niceties of an analogy of 'Forethought'.

King effectively prevented any serious consideration of the 'like' and 'unlike' ways in which revelation might be received and expressed in the narratives of Hebrews and Greeks and of all those stranger peoples then coming into the conversation of civilized folk. Those who were reared to read the New Testament stories as he was suggesting would, on encountering the new stories, ask only 'What are such stories like?' and hold themselves off from 'Are they like the stories I tell?', and most especially avoid 'What do these stories suggest that I am like?' But these were the questions which interested Handel.

In considering questions of narrative differently, Handel had some different things to say about predestination. King supposes that questions about predestination are bound to be about the 'election' and the 'curse and damnation' of Article XVII of the Thirty-nine Articles. Handel has a larger appreciation of the matter. The *Rinaldo* on which he was working in 1710, the year after King published his tract, is certainly concerned with the Christian fulfilment of destiny, but not with a destiny definable by the hero in terms of his individual salvation.

Handel and his librettist were so anxious that their audiences should understand that predestination was the central theme of their narrative that they introduced a character, Eustazio, whose only purpose in their design is to be there to sing an aria about an old hermit who has been given a knowledge of Rinaldo's destiny. In order to ensure that this aria was noted as an impressive intervention, they assigned the part of Eustazio to the popular castrato Valentini. He announced that the hero's destiny was written in 'the starry characters of Heav'n'. It is a destiny which is fulfilled in community. At the close of the opera, Rinaldo brings his enemies, the pagan general and the Levantine sorceress, to Christian faith.

Handel, equally topically, played out this story of predestination to evangelical happiness against a backdrop of the confrontation of European civilization and Asiatic wildness. Asia is the continent of Blackamoors in armour, mermaids singing, dragons spitting, and a woman who changes shape at will. It is the continent from which travellers have been returning with their tales. It is the testing-ground of Christian virtue. This is made absolutely clear at the very first appearance of the enchantress who dominates the action of the opera. She devotes her resources to the triumph of pagan Asia.

The problem of making a proper response to the intelligences being brought from strange places remained to trouble Europeans for the rest of the century, and was hardly solved by the practice of imperialism. But King's tract stirred minds for a short while only. So Handel, always sensitive to the moves of public interest, when he revived *Rinaldo* in 1717, excised Eustazio and the announcement of heavenly predestination.

Acis and Galatea and Esther (1718)

Until *Rinaldo* in 1711, Handel had exhibited no more than an educated gentleman's acquaintance with the tales that returning traders and missionaries were telling. He had begun Act III of the 1704 *Almira* with a masque of the Continents in which Europe competed with Asia for a lady's favour; in Rome, Cardinal Ottoboni had doubtless spoken to him about the libretto he had put together concerning the discovery of America; he had written a cantata *Nell'africane selve* for his Accademia patrons in (?) 1708; and in *Orlando* there is a part for an African prince. Not much else. But the importance of the tales from newly discovered cultures for British theologizing is not in their being foreign but in their stimulating reconsiderations of story. And all this while Handel had been thinking his way very carefully through the likenesses and the unlikenesses of myth, romance, history, allegory and emblematic figuring. He had, in Germany and Italy, been making music for each of them. When he arrived back in London, late in 1716 or early in 1717, he stepped into the British debate about these things with a pair of music dramas, one mythological, the other biblical.

By August 1717 he had settled into the house of James Brydges, Earl of Caernarvon, who had been Paymaster General of the forces in the wars with France and was soon rich enough to be created the first Duke of Chandos. If, as Swift remarked, 'all he got by fraud he lost by the stocks', the Duke remained extravagantly interested in music. He maintained a full choir and an orchestra of some two dozen servants for his chapel at Cannons, so that worship might be performed 'after the manner of the Chapel Royal'. For this Duke, besides his Chandos anthems, Handel composed in 1718 a reworked masque of *Acis and Galatea*, and the first version of his first English oratorio, *Esther*.

The chief musical difference between the Naples *Aci, Galatea e Polifemo* and the London *Acis and Galatea* is that for the Chandos performance Handel had the Duke's choir at his call. This effected the chief dramatic difference. The prejudice in the choral writing is all in favour of youth and beauty and frail joys of human loving. Nothing remains in *Acis and Galatea* of the ambivalent regard of *Aci, Galatea e Polifemo* for the constancy of the Cyclops. The shepherd chorus engages all our sympathy for the youngsters in their inevitable doom:

> Wretched lovers! fate has passed
> This sad decree: no joy shall last;
> Wretched lovers, quit your dream,
> Behold the monster Polypheme!

But if Polyphemus is removed from both the title and the centre of regard in *Acis and Galatea*, he is immediately present at this very choral entry. In its emphases we can hear the tread of the heavy-footed Polyphemus. The music of these ordinary human beings, with whom we identify in watching the action, is more Cyclopean than the Cyclops himself. In us, we have to acknowledge at this music, there are forces as irrational and frightful as in him. We too can be suddenly shifted from the cheerful moment of 'O ruddier than the cherry' into the jealous ferocity of 'I rage, I melt, I burn'. And the uncontrollable, erratic nature of such passion, as it is personally felt, is indicated by the *furiosi* markings of 'I rage' and 'I burn' being interrupted by the *adagio* of 'I melt'. This is 'verismo' writing.

Equally realistically, after the tragedy, the orchestra strikes up a lively dance tune for the finale. The inconstant chorus easily puts aside what has happened to the boy and his nymph. Through his reworking of a set of stage conventions to this cheerful ending, Handel reminds us that our emotions are really of very little interest to others. Few in his audience would have cared to be told that his sister, Dorothea Michaelsen, had died in Halle during the summer that he was writing *Acis and Galatea* for the Duke's evening party.

But Handel wanted to reaffirm, against the pessimistic verismo of the masque, a possibility of constancy in the lives of human beings. He took up the biblical account of the Jewish heroine Esther, not because he had 'sacred oratorio' in view, but because it seemed to offer an opportunity to celebrate the capacity of human beings to remain true to themselves, to keep faith with others, to sympathize effectively with those who suffer. Esther, by interceding with her husband, the irascible king of Persia, risks her own prosperity, even her life, to save her people from persecution by the king's wicked minister, Haman. Handel was treading very carefully here. He did not want to upset anyone. The story of Esther was not of any doctrinal importance to a Christian audience. If read at all by anyone at Cannons, it was as an historical romance with pleasing dashes of sex and violence. Handel was not yet thinking of public performance, otherwise he might have felt nervous that this retelling of the founding-narrative of the feast of Purim should disquiet his Jewish patrons; they made, later, a substantial section of his oratorio audience. Nor did he want to take any unnecessary artistic risk. He knew for certain that the story of Esther could be made into successful music. There had been an *Ester* opera by Nicolaus Strungk (1640–1700) at Hamburg in 1680, and an *Ester* oratorio by Alessandro Stradella (1638–82) at Bologna in 1695; and Handel may have read a new libretto made for another oratorio that Arcangelo Spagna (1631–*c*. 1725) published in Rome in 1706. He may also, when his concern for words is taken into account, be thought to have had greater confidence in this enterprise from knowing that the English libretto he actually set was derived, at a distance, from a play by Racine, the greatest dramatist of the previous age.

The Hamburg librettists employed by Keiser had been particularly fond of dignifying their profession by references to Racine. Handel would have known the alexandrine verses of Friedrich Bressand (*c*. 1670–99) and the less polished but more dramatically effective texts of Barthold Feind (1678–1721), both of whom made the outrageous claim to kinship with the great French poet. *Esther*'s libretto has its beginnings in a work by which Racine passed from classical to biblical narrative. He had been told by Madame de Maintenon that his *Andromaque* was not at all suitable for her girls to perform at the Maison Royale de St Cyr. Racine had thereupon obliged the great lady with a drama of another brave woman. In the preface to his 1715 translation, Thomas Brereton (1691–1722), who advertised his *Esther*, 'or Faith Triumphant', as 'with improvements from Racine', recommends the play as quite unlike those dramas which represented 'Abominations of the Pagan World'. But Racine had made *Esther* as Greek as he could. For the first time, he had brought a chorus on to his stage, contriving a number of occasions when comment might be sung to Moreau's music by the well-trained girls of Madame de Maintenon's school. Brereton concentrated attention on their 'diverse Psalms or Hymns; which to such as are especially inclin'd to Musick will have all the good effects of Modern *Opera*', without, he adds, 'any of its Absurdities'. He dedicated his play to the Archbishop of Canterbury.

Handel's librettist, who this time may have been Alexander Pope or may not, used Brereton's translation as a basis for the Cannons *Esther*. He was not too successful in transferring the dramatic structure of his original to this little oratorio. Another librettist might have reconstructed the tale of Esther until it was congruent with an *Acis and Galatea* paradigm. In *Esther*, as in the masque, a girl stands between a dangerous, uncertain, threatening power, and a weak but much-loved humanity. It is quite clear, however, that Handel did not feel that what he was offered in *Esther* was 'like' what he was offered in *Acis and Galatea*. Again, another librettist might have led him to appreciate the heroic and drastic queen as the fit prompter of some stirring music. The audience at the original school's performance had seen Madame de Maintenon herself figured in Esther, but in the text Handel was given none of the characters could be suspected of any similarity to anyone living or dead.

The anonymous librettist kept Handel from any exploration of 'Faith Triumphant', or of what it might cost a human being to remain constant in faith with others. Handel's dramatizing imagination could not be stimulated by such stuff as the librettist offered. He yoked a deal of *Brockes Passion* music to the *Esther* words and withdrew. Even the choruses, the most lively numbers of the oratorio, do not project the recognizably human excitement heard in the shepherd choruses of *Acis and Galatea*. Handel would require a more 'emphatic' version of a scriptural narrative before he could find a story he wished to tell.

Romance, Roman history and myth

The deist debate had shown that British Christians were unsure how biblical narratives were like and unlike other ways of telling a story, largely because they were unable to recognize a value in either their own or other people's story-telling. The libretto of *Esther* is a good example of their general inability to retell a biblical story so that it should declare the world they thought human beings inhabit, and the ways of inhabiting that are appropriate for Christians. So, as that first deist debate came to an end, Handel was resuming his own explorations of the clutches of stories more readily available to an opera composer.

On 20 February 1719, Handel wrote to the widower Michaelsen, who still oversaw affairs in Germany, that he had had to put off a planned visit to Halle because 'I find myself kept here by affairs of the greatest moment, on which (I venture to say) all my fortunes depend'. The new Royal Academy of Musick was being set up by English aristocrats under the leadership of the Duke of Newcastle, the Lord Chamberlain, and with the active financial encouragement of the King. They meant to ensure that Italian operas would be regularly performed during the London seasons. In May, Newcastle authorized Handel to travel around Europe engaging singers in one-year contracts. The ubiquitous versifier Paolo Rolli (1687–1767) was enrolled as secretary of the Academy, and he wrote the libretto for Porta's *Numitore*, the opening opera of the first season in 1720. Handel's *Radamisto* followed. He was at last started on a career of London opera. Between *Radamisto* and the *Imeneo* of 1740 he was to write 30 operas.

Radamisto (1720) and *Floridante* (1721)

Radamisto was derived by Nicola Haym from a Florence opera of 1712. The most interesting alteration of the original is in Handel's relocation of musical emphases from the disturbed relations of King Tiridate to the death-defying love of Radamisto and his wife Zenobia. Handel was sensitive to the demands of honour, and the ways in which these were jealously worked out as revenge in the *opera seria* conventions, and he gave these emotions full scope in his music, but throughout his career he welcomed whatever opportunities his librettists offered him to celebrate the self-sacrificing and creative wonder of a constant human loving.

Love, honour, jealousy and revenge are, at their intensest, the habitual occupation of the aristocratic characters of *opera seria*. That is what made these operas *serie* as opposed to the low-life comedy of the *opera buffa*. The plots of *opere serie* were, in order to accommodate as many of these huge passions as possible, replete with sudden reversals of fortune, alterations of affection, deaths, and the returns of those long thought dead. Handel was particularly adept at modulating from one situation to another in the course of a recitative before an aria. In *secco* recitative, the accompaniment was just about kept going in the *continuo* of harpsichord or cello. In *stromentato* recitative, it was more largely orchestrated. By one or other the composer was expected to keep the audience up to date with the twists and turns of the episodic story — 'This is what is happening to whom'. Handel is commonly more ambitious. His recitatives are designed as much for the revelation of character as for the acceleration of plot. They are often as strikingly original in their musical effect as in their dramatic. And they are usually shorter than those of the Italian *opera seria* composers. Handel understood that operas written or revised for production in England had to take account of the audience's incomprehension of the Italian language in which they were sung. Londoners did not care to be kept waiting in the recitative for the thrill of the aria.

The da capo aria for which his audience waited was an impassioned statement of an excited human being. It displayed both the bravura skill of the singer and the heightened emotion of the character: 'This is how I feel'. In Handel's operas, the hearer is brought by such an aria to the dangerous realization of a human sympathy with such a passion: 'This is how I could feel'.

The testing of vocal power in such an aria exactly paralleled the exhaustion of the situation. After the da capo repeat there was very little energy left in either the singer or the plot. The aria thus became the 'exit-aria'. The singer left the stage with as much applause as could be coaxed and squeezed from the audience, and the next recitative cleared the way for the onset of another passion in another voice. The aria thus did service for the close-up and the curtain fall. The audience had been brought into larger-than-life immediacy with the passion, and the release effected by their applause was a punctuation of the action. In Handel's London theatres the actual cloth curtain did not come down until the very end of the performance. It was part of the challenge to the management that they should produce a set of satisfyingly dramatic transformation scenes; it was part of the fun for the audience to see how cleverly the scene could be changed in full view. Only on a night when orchestra, singers and scene-shifters were all in good form could Handel hope for some in his audience to catch his meaning. Most especially was this the case when his librettist offered him so muddled a set of plot and sub-plot as that of *Floridante*. The complicated story of *Floridante* begins with a Persian king's breaking his word in order to possess a girl whom he has already promised to his victorious general. From this single act of tyranny all the complications derive. But whatever the muddles, disguises and baby-snatchings, we have to hold on to the central theme. Rolli dedicated his word-book to the Prince of Wales, confident that 'the Heroic lover' had been most vividly and feelingly celebrated in Handel's music. Handel had identified the source of whatever was interesting in this action as the general's certainty that, whatever his misfortunes, he will always be able to count on the love of the girl. The working-out of the plot through a series of ordeals for both of them leads to a crowning ceremony of that 'Constancy Triumphant' which was the title of the original work by Francesco Silvani from which Rolli had taken his story-line. After the difficulties he had had in clearing his way through the undergrowth of Rolli's plot mechanisms, Handel determined on achieving a greater freedom for his celebration of that constancy. He found appropriate scope for his large meaning in the text that Haym provided for the *Giulio Cesare in Egitto* of 1723.

Handel could rely on the audience for his Roman operas having some familiarity with his characters and his plot. *Giulio Cesare* is written for a society in which, while Shakespeare's *Antony and Cleopatra* might be thought a crude piece, Dryden had effected an elegant version of Cleopatra in *All for Love*. Handel's musical emphases would be the more acutely noted when he was treating such an element of shared tradition.

Giulio Cesare in Egitto (1723)

The libretto of *Giulio Cesare* has a rather more directly motivated action than many of those that Handel set. The story begins at the moment of Cesare's defeat of the army of Pompeo in Egypt. When Pompeo's wife Cornelia and his teenage son Sesto come to treat with the victor, Cesare promises reconciliation with the family of his enemy and a general peace. All the characters are young; Cesare is evidently in his twenties. They are very susceptible to the promptings of passion. Into their midst the Egyptian king, Tolomeo, throws the head of Pompeo: he has had the loser executed to ingratiate himself with the victor. Everything follows from this disruption.

The plot sets out two lines of action from the throwing down of the head. Cleopatra recognizes that she should be able to topple Tolomeo and get his throne for herself, and Sesto determines to revenge his father's murder. She will prove her womanhood by beguiling Cesare into assisting her political ambition. He will prove his manhood by killing Tolomeo. Both lines of the action are kept going until the very last scene of the opera. The sense of a satisfactory conclusion is perfectly achieved in the libretto when the removal of Tolomeo effects the re-establishment of a Roman harmony in which all the other characters may share.

Handel's music does not, however, keep to the scheme that Haym proposed. Handel was not interested in the boy's maturing sense of revenge, or in the girl's political management of the general. Handel had a meaning of his own, and he was discovering a range of dramatic skills at his command. He refused to develop the character of Sesto; each of the boy's four arias returns him to the same desire for revenge. The political theme is prevented from generating any intensity of emotion by the simple musical stratagem of giving Tolomeo no arias at all. But Handel develops Cleopatra's character through a sequence of eight arias. She begins her first aria in the happy confidence that her brother Tolomeo is a weakling and that Cesare will recognize this and dispose of him. What he does recognize is that she is lovely and lovable. Hearing the orchestra of her court, Cesare reckons it to be the music of the spheres, and fancies himself caught heavenwards in its wonder. This movement reaches its climax on Cleopatra's completion of the first section of her fourth da capo aria. Cesare delays the return with an exclamation of adoring love that convinces us all that she is indeed the mistress of the master of the world. Then, in a highly dramatic reversal, as if the opera itself had entered the second section of a da capo form, the opening expectations are halted by Cesare's defeat by Tolomeo's troops. Cleopatra's love for him is now heard, in the sixth aria, to be not simply an extension of her love for herself, her beauty and her ambition, but a fixing of affectionate value. 'Venere bella' has its minor complement in this cry of 'Se pietà'. As all hope is taken from her, Cesare reported killed, and herself in chains as the prisoner of her brother, her seventh aria registers in the most simple melody her tears of total loss, 'Piangerò!'.

Handel's presentation of Cesare most forcefully demonstrates his design of every element of the music, not only the arias, to bear the action along. If his management of Tolomeo through recitative alone was conditioned by the inadequacies of the castrato Bigonzi, the emphasis Handel placed on Cesare's accompanied recitatives was wholly according to his original design. Charles Burney (1726–1814) remarked that in *Giulio Cesare* 'both the composer and performers seem to have acquired even more reputation from the recitatives than the arias'. Handel's mastery of the recitative, and his sensitivity to the expectations that an audience would have of *opera seria*, enabled him to devise a sequence of surprising phrases. 'The modulation is so learned and so uncommon', as Burney again noted, 'that there is hardly a chord which the ear expects.'[14] Within these recitatives we hear Handel's development of his characters. Cesare himself becomes a master of music and thus a credible master of the world. 'Alma del gran Pompeo' shows that Cesare has no need of any dull slave to repeat *sic transit gloria mundi* in his triumphal cart. Handel's juxtaposition of military considerations and the sense of human fragility in Cesare's second great recitative is even more significant. Cesare escapes death in battle only to recognize his loneliness in not knowing what has happened to Cleopatra. The sense of the passing of all things human is made terrifyingly immediate as he views his dead soldiers on the battlefield. Handel's meaning is advanced in this recitative with staggering surety.

At the close of the opera, the aria movement of Cleopatra breaks in upon the recitative construction of Cesare. Cesare hears, amidst the dead, the call of Cleopatra's love. Love endures. And enduring, vivifies. Cesare summons energy, allies, troops, from nowhere, and rushes to rescue her. Cesare becomes 'the Heroic lover' that Rossi always knew him to be. Cleopatra's welcome declares that, as at the return of her own da capo arias, they now enjoy more fully, more excitingly, the life that they had enjoyed in their first experience of love. They all recognize the shared peace of the Empire as a context of liberation. Recitative and aria come together as the duet of constant lovers.

We accept this sudden twist of the plot not, as we accept the twists of the usual *opera seria*, because we only want to get on to the next musical sensation, but because we recognize a dramatic demand being worked out in the action. It is an appropriate culmination of events that Cesare should find new life. Love is heard in this music as a resurrecting power.

American savages

Once the language of 'resurrection' is invoked, questions of 'likeness' and 'unlikeness' occur again. How are we to estimate the uses of such a language in the contexts of myth and gospel and romance? When is it univocal and when is it equivocal? Handel had not taken up Keiser's scriptural example for his operas; and *Esther* was still looking like the dead-end for oratorio. But in his developing of *La Resurrezione* through romance and Roman history, Handel was again touching contemporary theological discussion. These questions of the values expressible in story, and of resurrection stories in particular, had been started again by the Jesuit missionary Joseph Lafiteau (1670–1740), who published in 1724 'a sort of eighteenth-century *Golden Bough*'.[15]

In this *Moeurs des Sauvages Amériquains*, Lafiteau was concerned to allege the Canadian Indian beliefs as evidence of some unanimous consent among peoples in witnessing to a Supreme Being. Bosman's African counter-evidence seems very meagre in comparison with the vast heap of American witnesses that Lafiteau piles up to demonstrate a primitive monotheism. Lafiteau is a generous-minded man. He hopes to learn from the Indian: 'One should study manners only to form manners, and a man will find everywhere something from which to draw advantage'. Lafiteau, in this more like Toland than Stillingfleet, is working to prove that the Indian religion is, like the Hebrew or the Egyptian or any other, a peculiar form of the original revelation and of the original human response to that revelation. All religions 'share the same principles and the same bases'. Each is 'holy in its origins'. However curious his comparisons, however patronizing his discernment of vestiges, Lafiteau is clearly a man of appreciative taste. He could not talk of the 'absurdities' of other people's beliefs, or of 'Superstition'. He reverenced every story that the Canadian Indians told him.[16]

Nevertheless, Lafiteau, alongside those others who were publishing accounts of other societies, was unintentionally helping to persuade the 'Generality' that not only could Hebrew and Christian stories be put into real relation with other versions of divinity, but that every revelation was merely a story made up by human beings. Those who encounter the Nootka story of the Salmon people's rise to a new life each year, or the Yurok belief in the return of the deer spirits in new bodies at the hunting season, will not necessarily enjoy a larger faith in the promise of resurrection in Christ, or a greater sympathy with that declaration of a power of love by which Caesar is recalled from the dead.

Admeto (1727)

It was with the more direct representation of the nexus of love and resurrection in Greek story-telling that Handel was concerned in the *Admeto* of January 1727.

The libretto for *Admeto* was derived, probably by Haym, from a Venetian original of 1660, *L'Antigona delusa d'Alceste* by Antonio Aureli, by way of a version made by Ortensio Mauro for a Hanover production in 1681. Aureli had thrust a comic sub-plot into the mythic action. The great story of Alcestis accepting death in the place of her husband and being herself brought back to the living by the prowess of Hercules had been distastefully yoked with an anecdote about Admetus' wooing of the princess Antigona while his wife was in the Underworld. The English librettist at least removed the embarrassing complications arising at Alcestis' return by making Antigona a *generoso rivale* who surrenders all rights in Admeto. Thereupon, like Jacquino in Beethoven's *Fidelio*, another story of a wife's devotion to a husband, a waiting admirer of Antigona begins to hope that she will marry him on the rebound.

Handel's music certainly declares his interest in the elements of the classic myth. The story of Alcestis is moved forward with enormous energy from the opening moment when we discover the dying Admeto in terror as bloodthirsty spirits come to seize him into the dark world below. These are the Grecian originals of the Furies of *La Resurrezione*. It is a measure of Handel's maturing command of such things that the overture to the second act which presents an image of Hercules' descent into that dark world is not an anticlimax but an intensifying of the terror. It may be that Handel was ignorant of classical drama, but I do not see any reason for our assuming this. He had had a very good schooling in Halle, had met a number of the most learned gentlemen in Europe at the Medici court and the Roman palaces, he had conversed with Pope at Cannons and, maybe, with Bentley at Kew. His chances of being introduced to Aeschylus and Euripides had therefore been several and various. And at Grimani's vice-regal lodgings he would have met young Neapolitan lawyers who had, like Alfonso Liguori (1696–1787), been taught to appreciate the story of Admeto as a work 'of human imagination' which prompted a rereading of narratives which were 'of faith'.[17] So it would not have been surprising if Handel had responded with little enthusiasm to the degradations of the myth proposed in the operatic sub-plot. But his dramatic genius brought the nonsense of Antigona into an instructive relation with the wonder of Alcestis. Antigona, too, is enabled to bear Handel's meaning.

The conventions of the old Venetian opera houses suggested that boy having lost girl will inevitably meet another girl. It is part of Handel's purpose to test the potencies of these conventions. Having to make arias of equal musical and dramatic excitement for the two rival soprano stars of the Haymarket theatre, Faustina Bordoni and Francesca Cuzzoni, Handel makes the confrontation of their two voices into a figure of the confrontation of a death-defying human love and the conventional wisdom which cannot acknowledge the possibility of such integrity.

Alcestis comes back from the dead to see her husband with Antigona. But, in this opera if not in *Acis and Galatea*, whatever decree fate has passed, love may outlast. The psychological interest of the opera is thus centred on Admeto. How much reality can humankind bear? With which of them, the noble Alcestis or the comfortable Antigona, will he choose to live his life? The castrato Francesco Bernardi, known as 'Il Senesino', who, rather unaccountably, has not given *primo uomo* the pejorative sense of *prima donna*, must have been well pleased to have a part which drew each member of the audience to identify with him. It would be impertinent to deem ourselves identifiable with Alcestis. It would be odd if we allowed ourselves to be identified with Antigona. But the Admeto of *Admeto* is each of us to the life. From the opening 'Orride Larvae' and its violent revulsion from the terrors of the grave, we accept that he is one of us. We feel with Admeto. When Antigona gracefully surrenders her clàim, we are relieved that he has been let off the hook. That shared revulsion and that shared relief indicate what Handel is managing through this story-telling.

When kings and conquerors come on the stage, their wigs and costumes declare their political importance. When they start to sing, the da capo aria declares the importance of their emotions. History and romance elevate a certain class of person. But myth is not class-conscious. Myth announces that, even if our lovings and ragings are not likely to make headline differences in the world, they still have meaning. Our ordinary lives are not insignificant. It is to myth, therefore, that Handel, in his effort to disclose meaning, directs our attention.

Stillingfleet had, characteristically, supposed that 'the memory of Jacob's long peregrination and service with his uncle Laban, was preserved under the story of Apollo's banishment, and being a shepherd under Admetus'.[18] It was more usual for Christians to see a prophetic resemblance in Hercules, the strong son of Jupiter. The story of Hercules' descent into the Underworld to bring back Alcestis seemed to afford an extraordinary likeness with Christ's harrowing of hell and his bringing back the faithful patriarchs to resurrection life. The likeness which had occurred to Clement of Alexandria (*c.* 150–*c.* 215) was enthusiastically taken up by Eustathius of Antioch (*c.* 280–*c.* 330) and Fulgentius of Ruspe (468–533), and was kept going by various patristic commentators. Those who were not Christians saw this likeness too. Celsus, in the second century, wondered if the Christians had not been historicizing their Herculean figure of Christ from the Greek myth. More ecumenically, the Emperor Alexander

Severus was said to have kept statues of Hercules and Jesus side by side on the altar of his domestic chapel. There had been a revival of these ideas in Renaissance literary theology. Boccaccio's *Della Genealogia degli Dei* (c. 1360), Chaucer's rather awkward translation (c. 1385) of Boethius's *De Consolatione Philosophiae*, Salutati's *De Laboribus Herculis* (c. 1450), Bonus' *De Vita & Gestis Christi* (1526) and Gyraldi's *Ercole* (1554) each had a share in making the likeness of Hercules and Christ receivable by educated Christians until, as Ronsard observed with entire seriousness in his *Hercule Chrestien* (c. 1560), 'everything which is written of Hercules ought to be read only of Jesus Christ'. Or, as the Scotsman Alexander Ross put it in his *Mystagogus Poeticus* (1647), 'Our blessed Saviour is the true Hercules'.[19] Handel may not have read these authors, but he felt their effect in the conversation of civilized Italians and Britishers, and he had certainly read Milton, who was the conscious continuer of the tradition. Milton had employed just this typological connection in *Paradise Regained* and in both *Samson Agonistes* and the 'Nativity Ode' which Newburgh Hamilton raided for verses to supplement the text of Handel's *Samson*.

That Handel was invoking in *Admeto* a typological tradition that was still very much alive for his contemporaries is shown by his opera's appearing in the very year that Andrew Ramsay (1686–1743) published his charming *Travels of Cyrus* in which he went much further than earlier commentators in exploring the myth of the heroic rescuer.[20] Ramsay, like Toland, wants to be taken for a reasonable man, and, like Lafiteau, he hopes to demonstrate the single principle of all religious activity. 'Men left to the Light of their Reason alone, have always looked upon moral and physical evil as a shocking Phenomenon in the Work of a Being infinitely wise, good, and powerful.' The contemplation of evil must lead, Ramsay thinks, to our reasoning out that we cannot have been like this from the beginning. Human beings become aware that they are 'degraded' for some fault. From this they reckon themselves 'exiles' from a better life. They start to hope for a recall to that life. 'All things', they tell themselves, 'are to be restored to their proper Order.' When Ramsay declares that the present, the past and the future, those 'three States of the World', are known not only by reason but by 'tradition', he is thinking first of a tradition of story-telling. All the poets, he says, of the Greeks and the Romans declare that they live not in the first age, which is of Gold, but in a second age of Iron, when moral and physical evils overflow the earth, and that they wait for a third age, when everything shall be 'restored to its primitive perfection'. They sing 'on all occasions' the exploits of a 'Son of Jupiter' who will descend, live among men, and rescue them from every enemy. The names of the Son may be many — 'Apollo' and 'Hercules' come to his mind — but the rescuer is always 'some Son of Jupiter giving Battles and gaining Victories'.

This classical paradigm allows Ramsay to frame a thesis that will cover a wide range of religion and story-telling. He turns with some confidence to 'examine the Egyptian Mythology' for signs of this rescuing Son. He finds them. Rational piety allows Ramsay first to translate Osiris into a figure of 'whatever there is in Nature well disposed, well regulated, good and perfect'. He is the Lord of the first age. From this it does not take much intelligence to work out what is going on in the story of Horus. Ramsay is already off to another country: 'Let us pass into Persia'. Plutarch had allowed himself to speak of Zoroastrianism's proclamation of two original and eternal gods working against one another, and of Mithras coming later to mediate in their cosmic warfare. He had thus muddled the paradigm. Ramsay therefore consults 'the famous Dr Hyde, a Divine of the Church of England', who has travelled in the Levant, learnt the language of the place, and produced a book in which he clearly states that 'the first Magi did not look upon the two Principles as coeternal', but believed that Darkness came later on the scene and was to be defeated by the Son of Light. The doctrines of the Magi fit precisely. And, as 'the doctrine of the Persian Magi is a sequel of the Doctrine of the Indian Brachmans', Ramsay goes on to consult the Vedam, which, 'though its antiquity is not perhaps so great as they affirm it to be', yet contains a very ancient lore. There he finds everything 'agreeable to the Greeks'. Indeed he would 'hardly have thought these Traditions authentick' or have brought himself to trust the Vedam as a witness to what had been believed in the earliest times, 'if this doctrine had not been perfectly agreeable' to what the Greeks had been saying. More of a like reassuring character was to be discovered when he applied himself 'to the Chinese books'. He feels secure in affirming that all religions witness to a Nature, exalted, fallen and redeemable, and to a Hero, who will accomplish this redemption in obedience to a heavenly Father. Everything has been pointing to the Christ.

What, 'left to the Light of their Reason alone', human beings have 'always' concluded, what 'all poets' have sung 'on all occasions', Ramsay would have discerned at a performance of *Admeto*. The once-upon-a-time happiness of wife and husband, the collapse into death, the rescue by a 'Son of Jupiter', would have sat patient at his comment. *Admeto* would have been simply a confirmatory exemplar of what he had known to be always the case. However interested Ramsay was in mythology, he was insensitive to the particular myth. *Admeto* is not, in Handel's creative understanding, simply another example of the 'three States'. It is an enquiry into relations being set up between the persons of the story, and then between them and the members of an opera house audience. Handel is suggesting that we ponder a relation between myth and our own ways of living as we attend to the faithfulness of Alcestis.

It was his own constancy in a fickle world that Handel laid before Parliament in February 1727 for gracious recognition. The petition for his 'naturalising' refers to Handel's 'loyalty' and 'fidelity' to the King's family, and to his having 'constantly' professed the Protestant religion. The approval of Handel's Britishing was one of the last official acts of George I, who died suddenly on a visit to Hanover in July 1727. George II at once forgot how his hated father had been Handel's patron, and, passing over Maurice Greene, his official Composer of the Chapel Royal, put Handel in charge of the Coronation music.

FROM *PARTENOPE* (1730) TO BUTLER'S *ANALOGY OF RELIGION* (1736)

Archbishop Wake, perhaps still a trifle irritated by Handel's rebuff in the matter of choosing the biblical texts, noted in his service book: 'the Anthems in Confusion; All irregular in the music'. Perhaps he had jotted this down during the rehearsal. The Coronation Anthems were generally held to be a huge success. 'The Admiration of All the Audience', as the *Norwich Gazette* reported on 14 October 1727. Handel did not, however, respond to this popular admiration by taking up further scriptural texts in English. He was still thinking of making his meaning known through Italian operas. He made another Egyptian piece for the 1728 season; *Tolomeo* did not, however, take.

He was in Italy again in February 1729. He had gone in search of new singers for his Haymarket company. Shaftesbury recorded that 'when in Rome, Mr Handell waited on his old Friend Cardinal Ottoboni, who received him with the greatest marks of Friendship and Esteem'. Mainwaring added that Handel would also have called on Cardinal Colonna but for His Eminence then having the Stuart Pretender as his guest. On his way home, with several contracts in his pocket securing Neapolitan and Venetian singers for his next season, Handel called on Michaelsen in Halle, and some of his old acquaintance in Hanover. He did not this time stop at Düsseldorf. The

Elector Palatine who had befriended him was now dead. Perhaps Handel had waited on the Electress at her father's court in Florence to which she had returned as a widow in 1717.

He worked all through the summer months as usual. When the new season opened he was ready with *Lotario*. It made him no money at all. His second offering was the altogether more interesting *Partenope*. Handel made anti-heroic fun of his own operatic conventions in this handling of the home life of Naples' legendary queen.

Partenope (1730)

In *Partenope* Handel is edging forward to discover if he is able, by translating myth into romance, to make a livelier impression of relevance. There is a line of exploration from the resounding declaration of love as a revitalizing power in *Giulio Cesare*, through the mythic representation of that power in *Admeto*, to the cheerfully familiar frame of reference of *Partenope*. Handel is deliberately lightening the tone in this opera. The myth has been translated first into a piece of European history, and then from the pomposities of *opera seria* into a set of dance tunes and military marches that should encourage a little foot-tapping. This is a music intended to touch the domestic lives of Handel's audience.

But the plot, even when gently self-mocking, is still that of the romantic *opera seria*. The faithful Rosmira of *Partenope*, who has been abandoned by Arsace in his infatuation with the tempestuous queen, is a more familiar figuring of the Alcestis of *Admeto*. She is not asked to give up her life for her love, but she does give up her identity. She has to disguise herself as a man at Partenope's court. Having to watch Arsace's wooing of the queen, Rosmira is placed in just Alcestis' circumstance when she had to watch Admeto with Antigona. The pressures of reality are felt in a trio of Rosmira, Partenope and Arsace, in which each voice refuses to chime with either of the others. The formal patterns of *opera seria* are being forced to accommodate the muddle of human feeling. Rosmira's faithfulness brings her to a crisis when, challenged by the unwitting Arsace to strip for a fight, she must drop all pretences and rely only on her constant womanhood. There is both the stuff of farce and a most touching delicacy in this moment. Handel wants his audience to recognize the deep-down freshness of such a love, and to feel through the romantic fictions a sympathy which will affect their dealings with others.

Ever the composer's loyal friend, Mrs Pendarves had blamed Handel's audience for the failure of *Lotario*: 'The opera is too good for the vile taste of the town'. But she noted that Handel was demanding an unusual attention to his meaning: 'The present opera is disliked because it is too much studied'. All the public wanted was a set of minuets and comic ballads. *Tolomeo* had been quite unable to compete with *The Beggar's Opera* at Lincoln's Inn Fields. Even *Partenope* proved to be 'too much studied' for the Londoners. It could not see off the challenge of *Hurlothrumbo* at the Haymarket, in which Samuel Johnson took the lead 'sometimes fiddling, sometimes dancing, and sometimes walking on stilts'.[21]

It may be that Handel's audience was so determined not to learn anything new about their ways of living that when they discovered that the characters of his operas, perplexed, ridiculous and sad, were intended as representatives of themselves, they refused to listen. But however great the temptation for Handel's friends to blame his audience for a failure, it should have been resisted. Handel aimed to entertain. He had not been successful lately. *Admeto* had had nineteen performances in the 1727–28 season, but *Tolomeo* and *Partenope* had neither of them managed half that number. He must have begun to fear that he had lost the knack of pleasing a London audience.

They may have been in no mood to be jolted from their habitual ways of thinking and doing by some Grecian hero, or Egyptian prince, or the courtiers of a Neapolitan queen. Just after Handel had proposed the disturbing reference of *Admeto*, Ephraim Chambers had brought out the first edition of his *Cyclopaedia* (1728), with a reassuring article advising readers just how they should abstract a comfortable moral from the 'feigned narration' of Greek story-tellings. In the very year of *Tolomeo*, Samuel Shuckford, on his way to adding another Norfolk living to his collection, had achieved wide fame with his two-volume *Sacred and Profane History of the World* (1728), in which the ancient Egyptians had been demonstrated to have invented their dynastic histories. And in any year, Georgian gentlemen who took a box at the King's Theatre, largely indifferent to questions of orthodoxy and heterodoxy, were hoping to avoid being given a 'Neapolitan favour' by the doxy waiting at the corner of the street.

Whether or not London audiences were frivolous in their resort to escapist musicals, whether or not they were wilfully resisting the foreign exemplars of human being that Handel was providing, London theologians had for a decade been marginalizing anyone who argued for some enlargement of Christian sympathy to those who were at all unlike themselves.

In 1720 Toland was complaining in *Tetradymus* 'to what sneaking equivocations, to what wretched shifts and subterfuges' intelligent men were forced to take themselves 'merely to escape disgrace or starving' at the hands of the Establishment. At the close of the decade, Thomas Woolston (1669-1733), an Origen scholar who wanted to allegorize the gospel accounts of Christ's miracles, was in prison for the offensive sound of his *Six Discourses* (1727-29) on pious ears.

In between, Establishment divines had been affronted by the insistence of William Wollaston (1659-1724), in his *Religion of Nature Delineated* (1722), on the miseries endured by most of the race for most of the time. Wollaston had been walking at night in the London slums. But nothing in the present condition of the poor of their city like the sweaty fear of sudden death in *Admeto*, the menace of rape in *Tolomeo*, the bitter domestic rows in *Partenope*, was to upset the comfortable logic of their theologizing. The theologians did not want to hear, after all King's precise talk of 'Wisdom' and 'Forethought', that the history to which mankind has been predestined is 'little else but the history of uncomfortable dreadful passages', and that 'the greater part of it, however things are palliated and gilded over, is scarcely to be read by a good-natured man without amazement, horror, and tears'.[22]

Nor did they want to hear anything more about those distant savages who had proved so disturbing to their assumptions during the course of the first deist debates. They had no wish now, whatever Arthur Ashley Sykes (1684-1756) was suggesting in his 1725 *Essay on the Truth of the Christian Religion*, to reconsider their judgement that the virtues of the distant pagans were nowhere near so valuable in the eye of God as the virtues of those who lived peaceably in a Christian country. The constancy of Handel's heroines, Alcestis, Seleuce and Rosmira, could not be a proper exemplar for English ladies. Sykes, having been severely reminded of the complexity of the orthodox doctrine of grace, was preferred into the decent obscurity of a prebendary of Winchester.

To those who had concluded that there was nothing to learn from any stranger, Handel must have seemed to be making operas at some great distance from the centre of intellectual discussion.

It was, however, just this sympathy with all sorts of persons within a common response to revelation and a common exercise of virtue that Matt Tindal (1657-1733) was expounding as the essential element of true religion in *Christianity as Old as the Creation*. The publication of this provoking thesis in 1730 set off the second series of deist debates in Britain.

In the *Partenope* of that year, in which the *Admeto* myth had been domesticated along with the romantic notions of history that propel

Tolomeo, Handel presented Londoners with that existing kingdom of Naples over which Austria and Spain were then squabbling. The British had their interest too. They would, in 1733, sign away that kingdom's future by the Treaty of the Escorial. Handel was, not altogether articulately, putting to his audience that events in a kingdom existing in their own days might have not only an historical context but a significance declarable in the forms of myth. By inference, events in their own lives might have such a significance. He was not ready, when writing *Partenope*, to make that suggestion plainly. But by bringing together, in the universal conventions of *opera seria*, a Greek myth, an ancient Egyptian romance and, in *Lotario*, a history of the Lombards, with *Partenope*'s legend, he was indicating that each narration had reference to the one shared condition of humanity. Handel was, by the start of 1730, occupying the ground over which the professional theologians found themselves disputing.

'The common Rights of Mankind'

Tindal's book is in great part devoted to the development of a notion which had occurred to Toland. Since God wills the salvation of the whole race, and that salvation is revealed in Christianity, whatever is necessary in Christianity must have been revealed to the race at all times of the race, and everywhere. Tindal writes in this context of 'the common Rights of Mankind'.[23]

It follows that anything which has been held as revealed only at certain times or in certain places must, however true, interesting or beautiful, be regarded as inessential. 'True Christianity is not a Religion of Yesterday, but what God at the Beginning, dictated, and still continues to dictate, to Christians, as well as to Others.'

Tindal understands that if the kind of thing Sykes has been saying about the community in grace of pagan and Christian is to be tested, theologians will have to look again at the evidences of paganism. He has been reading the literature of comparative religion, and has accepted a great deal of the analysis that men like Stillingfleet have been offering. Egypt is for him, as for them, 'that Mother-land of Superstition'. But he has also been attending to 'the Chinese books' of Ramsay. Tindal applauds the 'plain and simple Maxims' of Confucius. So much plainer than the parables of Jesus. He seconds 'Monsieur Libnitz' in his estimate of the morality of 'the Infidels of China'. So much to be preferred over that of 'the Christians at present'. He is ready to search the Scriptures.

He does not think it at all difficult to tell what is of yesterday and what is from the beginning. It is simply a matter of exercising a sensitive attention. Tindal is proposing an aesthetic discernment of spirits: 'A Mind that's attentive can as easily distinguish fit from unfit as the Eye can Beauty from Deformity, or the Ear Harmony from Discord'. And there are indicators already set up in the Scriptures as to how we should proceed. He notes a number of biblical hints at the inessentiality of moral law. He has a nicely prurient reference to incest, pointing out that what was a duty in the children of Adam is condemned in our Christian society, but may yet, if siblings find themselves alone on a desert island, be allowed again, even commanded. Again, both Testaments are severe in condemnation of usury, but reasonable orthodox persons must admit that to forbid usury in contemporary society would itself be immoral since without it industry would be discouraged, art unimproved, and trade destroyed. And Tindal, who often helped himself to rather more food at the All Souls table than the other Fellows thought polite, noted with relish that the strict command against consuming blood need not now persuade an Oxford don to abstain from black pudding.

In his more extended analysis of the alien character of the biblical stories and the morality they are said to enjoin, Tindal looked carefully at what, besides incest, was happening in the very first days of the race. He remarks that theologians who insist on 'the original Dignity of human nature' make no objection when 'the sacred story' presents us with a pair who 'came into the world in every sense Naked', not dignified at all, destitute even 'of that knowledge Experience gave their Posterity', and silly enough not to heed a divine warning against eating fruit that was bad for them. Whatever theologians may mean by 'preternatural gifts', in this story Adam is less competent in the use of reason than the pagan or the savage. Tindal enjoys another naughty moment when he alleges that the only faculty that orthodox theologians have thought it safe to say Adam had and we do not was that of erecting his penis at will. The heathen philosophers, whom orthodox theologians rate as unable to entertain a dignified enough notion of humanity, might be puzzled by such a version of dignity. They would be amazed, too, that our race's destiny depended on a conference between a woman and a talking serpent, 'even before Consent had giv'n any meaning to Sounds', that the original pair had been 'asham'd to be seen uncloth'd by one another', and that they had, most conveniently, 'all things necessary for sewing' on their determining to put on aprons.

What morality is taught by a narrative in which 'an infinitely good God cou'd permit a most malicious cunning Spirit to work on the

Weakness of a Woman, just plac'd in a new world', and who then revenges her fault 'on all their innocent posterity for ever'? Heathen philosophers would not be alone in querying such a story. Tindal makes his appeal not only to Confucius but to the savages of Lafiteau. He refers to 'the poor Indians' of the Americas who demand of the missionaries why a God who loves mankind permitted the Devil such scope. 'With us, One who does not hinder a Mischief, when it is in his power, is thought not much better than he who does it.' The whole race must revolt at such a sorry account of the Deity.

The biblical story is evidently a human invention. And not the invention of a very nice human being. There is no 'historical character' to the narrative, and no 'practical morality'. In this, the Fall story is a paradigm of the 'revelations' that the Hebrews have been putting about in their 'histories'. Tindal was particularly incensed at the Jewish claim that God instructed their ancestors first to deceive the Egyptians and then to kill the Canaanites. He does not need to read further in the Jews' account of themselves to know that 'as they were the most superstitious, so they were the most cruel' of the ancient peoples. His outrage against the Christians who have taken up so many of the Jewish stories for their own tradition is expressed more guardedly. But the conclusion is the same. These biblical stories, being so evidently the inventions of a mean and uncivilized people, have no relevance for those who would establish a religion of sensible men. King's attempt to employ analogical predication to extract some reasonable morality from the Old Testament narratives is demonstrably misconceived. Tindal is confident that he has proved that Scriptures must be left aside if a human being is to do the truth.

Those who made a direct response to Tindal were, generally, quite ready to accept his linkage of reason and conduct as encompassing most of what they meant by 'Christianity'. The dissenter James Foster (1697–1753), in his *Usefulness, Truth and Excellency of the Christian Religion* (1731), admitted Tindal's principle that any revelation had to be criticized by the instruments of human reason. He merely expressed an opinion that since pagans and Roman Catholics were so unreasonable, and uneducated, as to believe in doctrines of sacrifice, something must be given to show such persons what others had been able to see by 'the Light of Nature'. His Establishment friend, John Conybeare (1692–1729), in a *Defence of Revealed Religion* (1732), went further in his analysis of the uneducated, affirming that the varieties and extents of possible knowledge were so vast that every human being must be reckoned uneducated. We have all a need of revelation in order to identify the reasonable thing to do. Revelation helps us to see the moral landscape, he suggests, rather in the way a telescope helps us to see the distant prospect of a gentleman's estate. Adam and Eve in their Garden were given a revelation of just this sort; their mistake was to think that they could investigate the trees at their leisure.

Only in the works of William Law (1686–1761) was Tindal confronted by a logic which had its beginning not in human reason and conduct but in the overwhelming wonder of God. His *Case of Reason* (1731) works from the assumption that 'it is certain that the rule by which He acts must in many instances be entirely inconceivable by us, so as not to be known at all, and in no instances fully known or entirely comprehended'. We cannot reason to what is fit conduct for ourselves. We cannot decide for ourselves 'how sin is to be atoned'.[24] But even Law was no better than the rest of them in recognizing the peculiarly narrative character of the revelation of what had happened to Adam and Eve. Only Joseph Butler (1692–1752), sharing Law's sense of the inscrutability of life under divine governance, saw that there was something to be found out about narrative. Only Handel managed to find it out. But he came only slowly to appreciate what he could do with scriptural story-telling. He had to be nudged into oratorio.

The revival of *Esther* (1732)

Within a year or so of the publication of Tindal's disturbing book, Handel's friends were preparing an evening's entertainment which might have been expected to prompt his further consideration of the relation between those scriptural narratives that Tindal had discarded, the religion of sensible eighteenth-century men that he was advocating, and what Handel had himself been learning through his opera writing. They were organizing a private revival of *Esther* at the Crown and Anchor as a birthday celebration on 23 February 1732.

Bernard Gates, the Master of the Children of the Chapel Royal, arranged this treat, and brought along his boys to sing the choruses 'after the Manner of the Ancients'. Viscount Percival, who was of the company, evidently heard several terms being used in the gentlemen's conversation to describe what they were enjoying. He wrote that night in his diary of the 'History' of *Esther*, of 'this oratoria', and, again, of this 'religious opera'. Undecided as he was about the right term, he thought the piece 'exceeding fine'. He was a more indulgent listener than Archbishop Wake, referring only to 'some of the parts' being 'well performed'. Perhaps he and the company had been pleased by the musicianship of Master Randal, the Esther of the evening, who grew up to be Professor of Music at Cambridge. The gentlemen talked widely of their pleasing occasion. By 19 April some pirate concert-manager was announcing that *Esther*, 'an Oratorio or Sacred Drama', would be performed next day at York Buildings. 'Oratorio' now summons images of a very British and very dull presentation of worthy music by large numbers of decidedly amateur singers. But in 1732 'oratorio' was a strange new word, resonant of Italy, evening parties and fine voices. There was likely to be quite a crowd at this performance. And Handel would get no money at all for the unauthorized use of his music. He acted fast to make it a second-rate event.

Princess Anne, who retained an admiration for the man who had taught her to play the harpsichord, suggested that *Esther* be done at the King's Theatre in full operatic fig. It is likely that the unauthorized performance in April had been planned as a fully staged event; no other way of doing it would naturally have occurred to the manager. Handel, however, contented himself with a concert performance at the Haymarket on 2 May of 'the Sacred Story' of *Esther*, which was now advertised as 'an Oratorio in English'. The notice of this performance made it plain that *Esther* was not an opera: 'N.B. There will be no Action on the Stage, but the House will be fitted up in a decent Manner, for the Audience'. The advertiser went on to make the connection with the most popular of Handel's English biblical music: 'The Musick to be disposed after the Manner of the Coronation Service'. Presumably he was not drawing attention to Handel's raid on both 'Zadok the Priest' and 'My heart is inditing' in order to stiffen the score of *Esther* for this revival.

The Haymarket performance was most like the coronation performance of the Anthems in that it included Handel's most popular singers from the opera stage as well as the Children's chorus. According to Burney, writing his account of the Handel Commemoration in 1785, the Haymarket performances were given without 'Action' so that the Children of the Chapel Royal could be retained as the treble chorus. Bishop Gibson (1669–1748), Dean of the Chapel Royal, was so against operatic entertainment being confused with biblical narrative that he demanded that everything be done in concert fashion. Prime Minister Walpole was happy to acknowledge that the Bishop of London 'is my Pope and shall be my Pope', and, like Pope Clement in Rome, Gibson took a low view of Italian opera and of the houses in which such things were performed. He supposed that actresses, danseuses, castrati and their admirers were not the most morally improving company for his choirboys: he was probably right.

61

Not everything pleased everyone who saw *Esther*. The Italian singers made such 'rare work with the *English* Tongue you would have sworn it had been in *Welch*'. That judgement, however, came from one who thought Handel had been pulling a fast one by pretending his 'new Thing' to be anything other than 'Religious Farce'. To most of the London audience, Senesino was a great success as Ahasuerus, and Strada, despite 'a *Halleluiah* of Half an Hour long', a popular replacement for Master Randall. Royalty made up a family party for the first night, and returned several times during the run.

> Eager in throngs the town to *Hester* came
> And *Oratorio* was a lucky name.

Handel made a handsome profit. He seems, indeed, to have regarded the whole venture as a pleasantly money-making interval in his real business. By January 1733 he had an immensely innovative opera ready. An opera which, without reference to Scripture, related eternal truth to historical process in an exciting and convincing action.

The education of a hero: *Orlando* (1733)

For the libretto of *Orlando*, Handel had gone back to Carlo Capece, the wordsmith of *La Resurrezione*. Capece had extracted *L'Orlando, ovvero La Gelosa pazzia* from Ariosto's *Orlando Furioso* for Domenico Scarlatti's contribution to the Roman carnival of 1711. In the language of the 'argument' prefixed to the published libretto, this is an opera which 'tends to demonstrate the Imperious Manner in which Love insinuates its Impressions into the Hearts of Persons of all Ranks'. Through his musical organization of the story's crises, Handel tends to demonstrate that if such passion is indeed our common experience, it must command our common sympathy. Handel sees in this story of a man driven mad by jealousy an impulse for each of us, however insinuating the impressions of passion, to strive for an integrating virtue. What we share is not only the 'uncomfortable dreadful passages' of mankind's history which brought Wollaston to tears, but the graceful capacity for virtue that Sykes had been recognizing in the pagan. The hero survives the worst of mankind's experience to become the best of men. Each of us may yet convert such disintegrating impressions into an occasion of coadunatory virtue.

Orlando begins with the discovery of the magus Zoroastro, in meditation upon the mysteries of a divine order which are revealed in the stars. He is to teach such mysteries to the young prince Orlando. It is an oversimplification to term Orlando the 'hero' of the opera, since Handel shows that each of the characters, and thus, persuasively, each member of his audience, is capable of 'heroism'. The plot over which Zoroastro presides is driven forward by Orlando's disruptive desire for Angelica. Withstanding his advances, Angelica's constant love for Medoro is paralleled in Medoro's constant love for her, as he fends off Dorinda's passion. At the finale Angelica and Medoro are united, but that is as far as the *opera seria* conventions are allowed their scope. The happiness of the lovers is only to be obtained at the expense of Dorinda and Orlando. They should, according to the conventions, be recognized at the last line-up as the defeated villains of the piece. But neither shepherdess nor prince fits such a scheme.

The audience has heard Dorinda's gradual realization that she will never enjoy Medoro's affection. They have also heard that, in their happiness with one another, Angelica and Medoro have had sympathy for Dorinda's frustrated love. It is thus impossible for the audience to think of Dorinda as one of those scheming ladies whose sexual games provide the action of many an *opera seria* with its motive power. They are, to their surprise, to sympathize with an unhappy loser. They are to recognize the value of a human being who can stand aside in order that others may be happy.

Lest anyone in the audience suppose that such self-management could come easily, *Orlando*'s main action presents Orlando's schooling in the command of passion. Becoming a hero almost destroys the young man. Handel insists on the terrors that attend on any human being who would become an integrated person. Orlando goes mad, on stage. He imagines Angelica with Medoro and is at once in hell. Charon brings him to the flaming regions of Pluto and, as Cerberus barks at him, he sees Medoro being feasted by Proserpine. The man is in every woman's arms. As he rushes to slay his rival, the scene dissolves and he collapses into the real world of Zoroastro. His madness crashes through the formal patterns of recitative and aria, sending dance and march tunes, high notes and growls, scattering in the score. The excitement is immense; and Handel's control of the excitement is even more impressive. He shows the young man's struggle to regain control of himself. He shows that it can be done. The destructive forces within us, we know it feelingly, can be brought under the governance of virtue.

The conventions of *opera seria* have been wholly disregarded in Handel's presentation of Orlando's schooling. The very idea of a hero's having to learn, to mature, to come into command of himself, is entirely foreign to the ways in which librettists and composers had been trained to handle characters. In *opera seria* the hero *is* a hero, by definition, from the beginning, and always. The da capo aria through which his heroism is displayed always brings him back to being just what he always is. The villain *is* a villain, equally, but, unlike the hero, the villain may suddenly change his nature and repent if the plot demands this for the *lieto fine*. Orlando is not a villain. His conversion is not a sudden change to ensure that everyone lives happily ever after. He is the hero whose development is the continuing occupation of the opera. His history leads him to the accomplishment of heroic virtue.

As in *Admeto* and *Partenope*, that virtue to which the hero moves in *Orlando* is kept constantly before the audience in the unwavering faith of the heroine. Angelica remains the still centre of *Orlando*'s turning world. Her devotion to Medoro endures through every changing, threatening circumstance. The difficulties that surround her are real enough, but she persists in the virtuous affirmation of a love that, as it survives the final curtain, must surely prove eternal.

Orlando is thus the most successful attempt Handel has yet made to reconcile the demands of myth and history, eternal verity and temporal process. What is true 'always and everywhere' has proved to be expressible in the particularity of a time and a place. Handel is making his own statement in the discussions that were begun in Ramsay's comparative religion studies and given greater importance through Tindal's provoking thesis. In the midst of making this statement there came the theatrical crises of 1733, when a number of opera-goers were organizing an 'Opera of the Nobility' to rival Handel's company. He began to lose money at an alarming rate; he had to offer something new. Since myth, history and romance would occupy the rival stage as they were occupying his own, he made a quick dash to the last of Keiser's categories. Handel produced *Deborah* in March 1733. He revived *Esther* for April. And by June he had written *Athalia*.

Deborah and Athalia (1733)

Deborah was not a success. Quite apart from the natural disgruntlement of the subscribers at Handel's doubling the price of seats for the first night, the public was right to think this a very disappointing evening. Handel had not appreciated how much work needed to be done to make his oratorio form attractive; and his librettist had made a wholly understandable but disastrous mistake.

Sarn Humphreys (?1698–1738) was a sympathetic hack trying hard to shape *Deborah* into the sort of text that he thought Handel would find congenial. He was a well-liked member of the Cannons circle, eager to please, but not sensitive to what Handel had been doing since

Esther, in which he had had, perhaps, also some text-making part. Humphreys made huge efforts to wrest the story of *Deborah* from its original form as a heroic saga into a piece that should promote a meditation upon the fixed nature of human experience. Every time an exciting event seems about to move the action forward, Humphreys inserts a pause for reflection. In doing so he quite ignored the example of the 1732 libretto of Maurice Greene's *Deborah and Barak* which was certainly available to him. *Deborah and Barak* is far more biblical in its pace than *Deborah*: there is not a single delaying da capo aria in Greene's setting. Humphreys would have plundered the text if he had not thought that Handel wanted something more assertive of the fixity of things. His mistaking Handel's present temper is evident in the resulting music that Handel made for these meditative passages, which too often remains unlively and unlovely.

That Handel did not send Humphreys scuttling back to his desk to rewrite uncongenial parts of the *Deborah* text was not because he had any sense that it had literary merit. For each of the revivals between 1734 and 1756 Handel made cuts, alterations and insertions, with scant regard for Humphreys' verses. That he retained the meditations in 1733 indicates that he was himself not entirely comfortable with his new understanding. He had not yet discovered the satisfying expression for a scriptural coincidence of the historic and the mythic in our lives. But he was eager to try again. He sat down to work on the *Athalia* libretto that Humphreys had derived from Racine's *Athalie*.

Racine, in constructing *Athalie* for Madame de Maintenon in 1690, was far more daring in his retelling of the 2 Kings 11 story than others had been in making dramas out of scriptural subjects, more daring than the librettist of Stradella's *Ester*, for example, and far more daring than he had himself been in his reworking of the story of Esther. He concentrated the action of several years into one day of *Athalie*: the day of the counter-revolution of Jehoiada. In making the Hebrew chronicle take on the form of a Greek play, Racine was relying on his own theatrical success in establishing classical tragedy as the appropriate pattern for the dramatic expression of an important idea. But it is difficult to exaggerate the daring of his invention of character and motive to push the scriptural story along. Athalie herself, haunted by her past, always conscious of her royalty, ever looking to her dynasty's future, is a splendid creation from the scraps of information offered in 2 Kings.

Racine proves himself still the master designer of a drama in his structuring the relation of the old queen and the grandson who deposes her within an imposing declaration of the meaning of history. Athalie, at her first entrance, announces that she has had a dream of her mother, the infamous Jezebel, who had come to warn her daughter that God was lying in wait to destroy her. As, in her dream, Athalie had reached out to her mother, she had touched only the torn flesh and mangled bones that had been savaged by the Yahwists' dogs. And then, as she fumbled with this hideous mess, a boy dressed in the vestment of the Jerusalem Temple came to plunge his dagger in her breast. Waking in horror, she had rushed to the Temple. There, at the altar, she has just seen the child again. The boy in the vestment represents a divine promise being made to Racine's contemporaries. He is the innocent future. At the centre of his drama, Racine enables the priest Jehoiada to prophesy the workings of God's providence from the coming of the young king, and his crowning in Jerusalem, through the Babylonian captivity and the destruction of the Temple to the audience's own participation in the Kingdom of Christ. His review of salvation history reaches to the direct question of dramatist to audience: 'Do you find it so difficult to love God?'

Racine intended to shock his audience. Humphreys was not willing to take such a risk in London. He altered Racine's design so that *Athalia* should no longer reach forward. The historical line of 'salvation history' is supplanted by a closed circle of repetitive, Platonical phases of experience. Humphreys shortens the priest's prophecy so that it simply announces that Athalia is about to be replaced by the grandson he has kept hidden, and fits Joad out with a further aria in which God's relation to events is expressed as 'He bids the circling seasons shine'. The libretto of *Athalia* represents Humphreys' effort to express an ancient agriculturalist view of what is always true in the contemporary terms of the deist assertion of a Christianity as old as the creation.

That the oratorio does not have quite that effect is entirely due to Handel's counter-effort in the music. He dramatizes the ferocious vitality of Athalia, the charming simplicity of the boy, and the careful plotting of the priest Joad, so that we hear a different understanding of human being. But Handel could not in the end find his way out of Humphreys' closed circle. The final celebratory chorus brings back music first heard in association with a harvest festival. The last reference to political events, to human efforts towards changing their condition, is the music of the repetitive round of the seasons, and the observance of that round in the liturgical calendar. There has been, literally, a revolution. The political coup engineered by Joad is as 'circling' as the seasons; it puts things back where they would have been. All Athalia's activity has come to nothing. All his has come to what would have been.

Athalia was first performed at Oxford University's Publick Act, and was a great success. University people would have been readier than London merchants to accept a view of time based upon repetitive seasons: their year always began after the gathering of the harvest. But Handel was too intelligent and sensitive not to realize that, in celebrating the fixity of all that was significant in the universe and reducing human history to a pattern of circling seasons, he had gone quite against the tone of the biblical story.

The image of the eternal God

The difficulty of reconciling an historical revelation with the persistent truth about God and his creation returned to the centre of theological discussion in *Things Divine and Supernatural conceived by Analogy with Things Natural and Human* by Peter Browne (*c*. 1660–1735), which was published in 1733, the year of *Orlando*, *Deborah* and *Athalia*. Browne had been promoted to his see of Cork and Ross, as Toland never tired of boasting, on account of his ferocious attack on *Christianity not Mysterious*.[25] He now promised that he would deal 'with a Mungril perticoloured Generation of Infidels' who were falsely claiming to be Christian deists.[26] Browne may have heard rumours that Tindal, in his Oxford college conversation, had admitted that his form of deism amounted to little more than atheism. Browne knew what had to be said to these 'Atheists and Deists and Libertines'. Much of his book is a restatement of what King had been saying in his pre-destination sermon but Browne is aware of the recent shift in the tone of theological discourse. He is aware of the new interest in history. His rebuttal of Tindal's account of theological language demonstrates a concern even amongst divines of the most philosophical temperament that there has been a history not only to revelation but to the theologians' understanding of revelation. 'Analogy' itself has a history.

Browne begins, as Tindal had begun, with the Genesis story of Adam, which he takes to be the first simple attempt of the race to say what had actually happened in their lives. Deist suggestions of the story as a decadent version of some atemporal, reasonable and univer-sal truth, however plausibly supported by Ramsay's researchers, are put aside. Browne looks carefully at the language of Genesis for signs of the historical author's intentions. It strikes him that there is nothing in his account of the creation of other creatures which corres-ponds to the historian's assertion of 'our being made after the image of God'. The reduplication of the words 'image' and 'likeness' suggests to

Browne that 'something is intended very remarkable'. He cannot
suppose that 'only a Figurative' likeness is meant here. The 'image' is
not 'imaginary', it is the first member of an historical series. It is
a prescient justification for 'all those Sentiments, and Words, and
Expressions which thro' all Generations were Necessarily to be transferred from the Human Nature to the Divinity'. It is especially with our
intellectual capacity that this first historian is concerned, 'in respect of
which we are said to be made in the *Likeness* and after the *Image* of
God'. This is as it should be; it accords with the history of our personal
discernment of the proper language of theology: 'If the Reader will
look inward and think with some Intenseness, He will find that in
attributing to God our Bodily Members of Movements, or any other
things merely Material, he transfers the bare Words only, and abhors
the transferring of the Idea'. This abhorrence is a sign of his having
become aware that while he keeps his language to physicalities he is still
in the sphere of metaphor. But 'in attributing the Operation and
Perfections of the Mind or Intellect', the reader has learnt to transfer
'both the Word and the Conception without Scruple'. We come to such
a sense of appropriate attribution by inheritance: it bears the primeval
impression from the creation of intellectual beings in the image of the
divine being. Again attending to the language of Genesis, Browne
notes that the author told his story of our creation quite precisely.
Nowhere did he suggest that God is like us. The history of competent,
orthodox exegesis is alleged at this point in his argument.

Browne found Thomas Aquinas a particularly helpful exegete, for
Aquinas 'would have a particular Notice taken once for all', that
though the Creature 'may be said to be like God, as we say a Picture
or Image is like a Person it represents', yet 'it cannot be said with the
same strict Propriety of Speech, that God is like the Creature'. No one
would say that a man was like his portrait, so, Browne observes, no
one should say that 'the Original archetypal Perfections of God have
a Likeness of any Created Perfections'.

The distinction of the metaphorical, what is 'figurative', and the
analogical, what is 'intellective', for which Browne is constructing both
a scriptural and a psychological base has its dangers for orthodoxy. It
puts certain elements of the historical revelation at a disadvantage in
theology. If taken too precisely Browne's language might suggest that
scriptural talk of God having a right hand or of his walking tells us
nothing of God. Browne sees that he has to say something quickly to
defend the honour of Scripture. He transfers from the comparative
study of Hebrew and pagan stories that complacent notion of
decadence which had proved so useful to both the orthodox Stilling-

68

fleet and the unorthodox Tindal. He invents a history of religion in which the admittedly metaphorical language of the descriptions of God which occur throughout the Scriptures are said to be temporally later than the primary innocence of the analogical. The divine 'image' in human beings must not be thought to consist in a capacity to walk with God in the cool of the evening. And the perfect 'image' in Christ is not to be properly expressed in the 'Figure and Metaphor' of 'Door, Vine, Way, and Light'. The scriptural authors must, like the patristic and scholastic authors, like Browne, like the Reader himself, have thought their way through to an appreciation of analogies and then realized that they had to employ some arresting metaphors if their decadent hearers were to attend to the divine instruction.

The effect of describing such an historical process was to further persuade Browne's inexpert but interested reader that somehow the analogical reference of 'image' was more to be valued than the narrative in which the 'image' originally occurred. What had begun as an historically inclined account of analogical predication had ended in dismissal of those elements in Scripture which were most obviously historical: narratives of individual people and their actions were said to be irrelevant to the great matters of theology. It was, indeed, Browne's boast that in theology he had supplanted 'person', which he took to be infected with Arianism, with the orthodox 'essence'.

Browne's abstracting attention to the notion of *imago Dei* has abandoned the reader to speculations about the inadequacy of the scriptural story-telling for any disciplined account of God, and for any account of God's human image.

Handel would have found Browne's treatment of *imago Dei* rather thin. Halle had certainly offered a larger version. Francke's *Sonn-Fest-und Apostel Tags Predigten*, published in 1746, represents a fair selection of Pietist preaching in Halle 50 or 40 years before. In a sermon of 1689 on the feast of the Transfiguration, Francke elucidated *imago Dei* as a call of God to his women and men. Vocation begins with the realization of the wretched state of unconverted life, and proceeds in the recognition of the need to follow on the way of the Cross, and the enlivening promise of resurrection. Through *imago Dei* the Christian is brought to such a likeness with Christ that suffering has resurrection value. If there were to be, in Browne's congregation, any renewal of that sense of vocation which Francke was reading in *imago Dei*, there would have to be some preaching of the enlivening relation of the divine with human beings.

In *Athalia* Handel had worked within the terms of a Brownean view of reliable but unknowable divinity. Humphreys had offered him nothing more. Handel had also accepted the conditions imposed by Racine's estimate of the scriptural narratives. He had done what he could with a text which assumed that those narratives were written by men who had no interest at all in the people involved in the events; that the dramatist had, therefore, to invent temperaments and motivations to forward his own notion of the action. But it was no justification of the interest of 2 Kings to present thoroughly re-imagined figures of Athalia and Joad. The kind of dismissal of story effected in Browne's treatise could only be reversed by attention to some actual scriptural story-telling. The way forward from Racine's dramatic reinterpretation was to demonstrate how personal was the involvement of the characters in the action of the scriptural story.

The re-establishment of scriptural story-telling as of use in a human being's self-discovery and self-expression would have to be based on some reaffirmation of the appropriateness of stories generally for such enterprises. Only then could the peculiar use of the stories told in Scripture be propounded. To secure such an enterprise from Browne's accusation of 'theatrical Folly' would require some preliminary recouping of what had been suggested by *Admeto*, *Partenope* and *Orlando*. Handel turned for a while from the English, scriptural oratorio. He shaped his next story-telling into a fundamental question expressed in Italian, romantic opera. *Alcina* represents a man's confused search for his self.

Seeking a self: Alcina (1735)

The 1733–34 season in the Haymarket had not made money. Handel was personally responsible for the salaries of the singers he had hired, both the English and the Italian. He had to keep things going. And when his lease of the King's Theatre expired, he took his whole company off to the brand new opera house in Bow Street, Covent Garden. For the opening of his new season, he wrote a song and dance number for Apollo with his Muses and, staying with the Greeks for a while, cobbled some old music together for an *Oreste* to keep the customers happy until *Ariodante* in January 1735, and the second new opera, *Alcina*, in April.

The critic of the *Universal Spectator* noted that Handel had, in his 'beautiful and instructive' opera, shown how it is that 'neither the Council of Friends, nor the Example of others' can prevent 'giddy head-strong Youth from the Chase of imaginary or fleeting Pleasures'. But Handel was making a more complex statement than that.

Alcina is a version of the old Circe story. The beguiling enchantress Alcina lives on her magic island with her sister Morgana, guarded by a garrison under the command of her general, Oronte. She has the unhappy power of making men reveal what they are really like. The knights who come to woo her on her island find themselves turning into all sorts of unflattering forms: ferocious animals, fatuous plants, stolid stones, and inconsequential waves of the sea. Ruggiero, who is wooing her when the opera begins, has not yet lost his physical shape, but he has lost his knightly identity, for he has abandoned, forgotten, his true love Bradamante. The confusion within him is indicated in his first extended music: admitting he always falls for 'a lovely face', he asserts 'I am incapable of losing faith'. Bradamante comes with her guardian Melisso, a magus of the Zoroastro sort, to rescue her lover. To make her journey safer, Bradamante has disguised herself as a man. As in *Admeto* and *Partenope*, it is the heroine who is the hero of the piece. So entirely has he forgotten himself and her, Ruggiero will not believe Bradamante when she declares her true identity. He invokes the words for virtues which he no longer possesses. He talks of 'duty' and 'knightly courtesy' and 'loyalty', all now misdirected towards Alcina, as he pushes Bradamante away. He makes his final appeal to a power he feels excuses whatever he does: 'my fate'.

At every turn in his experience, Ruggiero thinks it enough to say that he is confused and that he is confused because he has been enchanted. Handel's music makes us ask why Ruggiero has been susceptible to such enchantments. It gradually becomes clear to the audience that Ruggiero is not a wholly unwilling prisoner on the magic island. 'Verdi prati', his serenade to the luscious lotus land, is the most powerful expression of his unacknowledged desire to stay within the dream world. He never truly knows himself: he cannot face up to the demand that love is making on him.

Our own confusion of what is truly desirable and what is 'imaginary or fleeting' is intensified when Alcina seems to have fallen in love with her captive. She has certainly fallen for a new image of herself. She feels, she says, Ruggiero's attempt to escape from her as a betrayal. She weeps. It is a moment of shock for the audience when they find themselves being brought by the music into sympathy with the sorceress. Her new image is kept up in self-sacrifice. Alcina brings the lovers together; all seems about to be resolved in just the way that the action of *Admeto* had been resolved. But Handel is not telling quite that story this time.

He confronts us with our own infatuation with the happy ending. Alcina, to our confused astonishment, makes another effort to separate Ruggiero from Bradamante. What excuse can we now make to ourselves that we have been so easily deceived? What confidence can we have in either our judgement or our virtue? Do we blame someone else? Blame the librettist and composer for tricking us? Comfort ourselves that it is only by the magic of such music that we could have been made to be so silly? At the close, smashing Alcina's urn in which her magic power was stored cannot, after such an anticlimax, seem more than a temporary expedient. Alcina will have to be driven off again. And again.

It was by an act of splendid theatrical imagination that Handel here brought the machinery of his Baroque stage into his musical design. It had always been a chief excitement of opera from the earliest performances in the Medici apartments that the engineers, builders, painters and candlemakers would conspire to produce some hugely elaborate set which should be capable of being changed into something rare and wonderful before the audience's very eyes. The 'transformation scene' of pantomime is the last remnant of this tradition. In *Alcina*, at the breaking of the magic urn, we ourselves see through the gauze of the enchanted palace, with its 'statues, obelisks, and trophies of many kinds' and its 'menagerie of wild beasts that pad back and forth in their cages'. All this suddenly disappears, with our illusions, and we are discovered in 'a vast subterranean cave' where 'many rocks now change back into men'. There is a visual promise that we may yet be free from self-deception. Handel's dramatic story-telling demands that we look into our own lives for its continuation.

Just before the end of his opera, Handel offers a positive image of that self-knowledge and self-government which he is celebrating through so many negative instances. He and his librettist had inserted a new character into Giuseppe Pulvini's 1728 version of the Ariosto anecdote, *L'isola di Alcina*. Handel assumes that the better sort in his audience will notice any alteration that he makes in an old piece and pay it particular attention. Oberto is important to him. The young man, dazzled by Alcina's deceits like the rest, wanders through the opera like Ferdinand in *The Tempest*, seeking his father Astolfo. He knows he is near him. 'How do you know?', asks Alcina. Words that meant nothing in Ruggiero's protestations come out sincerely: 'Because of fate . . . tears . . . duty'. The mocking Alcina leads Oberto to a cage of beasts. She lets a lion out. 'Kill it', she commands. But Oberto holds himself together. He governs his terror. 'Do not trust appearances', says Alcina when the lion looks at him in a friendly way. But the boy sees through her deceits. He recognizes his father within the lion's skin.

There is, together with the relation between instruction and the integrated self which the *Universal Spectator* had noted, a relation between nature and the integrated self. Handel is suggesting through *Alcina* that there is a liberating power in both education and untutored natural feeling, a liberation not only for the single self but for others. Melisso frees Ruggiero. Oberto frees Astolfo. Oberto is only in the opera to make this one point for Handel.

Tindal had been wholly convinced that the attentive mind would as naturally appreciate what God was declaring in the world as the ear would appreciate musical harmony. To discover oneself one had only to think clearly. But we live in a muddled and muddling world. There is a complexity in experience and a contrariety of emotion in the experiencer. The mind of the most attentive and reasonable human being may well be disturbed. *Alcina* figures such a disturbing circumstance and disturbed response. Ruggiero loses himself. Wollaston, on his night wanderings in the London slums, felt that an honest man must be 'very sensible how much he wants a guide' in the dark world. He thought Scripture to be that guide. Ruggiero's being brought out of his confusion by the art of the Wise Man, Melisso, corresponds to the work Wollaston thought that Scripture did in our lives. There was certainly an amount of agreement amongst orthodox and deists that Scripture gave practical instruction for getting safely through the alleys of the world. But there was also, within the tales of travellers and the speculations of philosophers, an increasing pressure to acknowledge a natural witness to the good life. In figuring this consideration in the Oberto incident, Handel is approaching a further significant shift in English theologizing. There was a contemporary excitement at the prospect of aligning Scripture and nature as declarers of the divine. Browne's 'analogy' and the more conversational 'like' were being brought into sharpest focus in the discussion of those relations shown by Melisso and Ruggiero, Oberto and Astolfo. What is intuitively reflected in *Alcina* was being professionally developed in the work of Joseph Butler.

Analogy, self and liberty

In 1736, the year he published his great work, *The Analogy of Religion, Natural and Revealed, to the Constitution and Course of Nature*, Butler was appointed Clerk of the Closet to Queen Caroline. He became a regular member of the Queen's pleasant seminar where divers men of learning, Newton, Bentley and Berkeley among them, were encouraged to give their opinions an airing. Butler would also have met the young curate of Kew, Thomas Morell, who was then annotating Locke's *Essay Concerning Humane Understanding* for the Queen, but was later to achieve a greater distinction as Handel's librettist for *Theodora* and *Jephtha*. And, even if he did not attend the Covent Garden gala for the wedding of the Prince of Wales, Butler very likely met the composer himself at St James's and Kew.

On the Queen's death, and to fulfil her recommendation, Butler was made bishop of Bristol in 1738, though he demurred a little at being offered the poorest diocese in England. It was not, however, until he had been translated to Durham, a very rich see indeed, that the famous 1758 performance of *Messiah* took place in Bristol cathedral, the only performance in a public church of an oratorio by Handel during his lifetime.

There is a famous anecdote, rather better authenticated than most of those about Butler, of a conversation with Prebendary Josiah Tucker concerning the occurrence of madness in human beings. As the gloom gathered in the rose garden, the bishop remarked that neither medical men nor those who search the Scriptures could determine the cause of madness.[27] Butler's considerations were taking him further than Handel had gone in *Orlando*. They were certainly taking him further than Prebendary Tucker wanted to go. He was appalled to be asked by his bishop, 'Why may not whole communities and public bodies be seized by fits of insanity as well as individuals?' Tucker wanted no part in such talk. He mumbled something about never having considered the matter. Butler opened the lid on horrors: 'Nothing but this principle, that they are liable to insanity, equally at least with private persons, can account for the major part of those transactions of which we read in history'. Any honest Christian's announcement of the revealed meaning of history must, on Butler's view, itself seem rather odd, in congruence with the oddity of events. Thus he says of his own exposition of the mediatorship of Christ that 'it may be thought that this whole manner of treating the subject' supposes mankind to be 'in a very strange state', and so, he says, it does, 'but it is not Christianity which has put us into this state'. T. H. Huxley once suggested that the principle of Butler's *Analogy* was that 'there is no absurdity in theology so great that you cannot parallel it by a greater absurdity in Nature'.[28] It seemed to Butler, rather, that nature and Christianity being both so strange may persuade us to enquire into the 'probability' that Christian teaching is in accord with what is going on in the natural world.

Toland had contrasted 'probable' with 'constant and necessary', allowing that 'in Matters of common Practice' we may 'sometimes admit *Probability* to supply the Defect of *Demonstration*', but this would be inadmissible in the conduct of a serious argument.[29] Tindal had been so emphatic about men's commonly 'mistaking the Degrees of Probability' that he too was taken to be insisting on the uncertainty of our practical estimates of life.[30] 'Probability' was being used in a campaign to undermine customary 'Certainty'. Butler, contrariwise, began from our usual estimates: 'That which chiefly constitutes Probability is expressed in the word Likely'.[31]

And in a world where 'strange difficulties have been raised by some concerning personal identity', Butler is eager to defend the 'probable' self. He loves life: its vigour, the persistence of living agents, of human persons. The final theme of *Alcina* is at the centre of contemporary debate. Butler takes a harder case than that of Oberto and the lion. He talks of persistence after dying.

He begins from a likelihood in nature. 'The change of worms into flies, and the vast enlargement of their locomotive power by such a change' and 'the general law of Nature in our species that the same persons should exist in different modes from period to period of their lives' provide the bases for an appreciation of the likelihood 'that we are to exist hereafter in a state as different (suppose) from our present, as this is from our former'. Personal identity persists throughout changes of physical or mental faculties. So death is likely to place us in a complex of relations 'in which our capacities and spheres of perception and action may be greater than at present'. We may enter, newly endowed with faculties fit for such a state, into the Kingdom.

It is with this sense of probable connections, of the likelihood of a consistent 'natural' law in our ordered cosmos, and of a higher sphere being like our present sphere, that it may be said that 'the Reign of God' is 'like' a farmer, a mustard seed, and a wedding feast. The affirmation of the probable is the first step to appreciating what is going on in the biblical story-tellings.

The deist habit of reading the Bible as one would read any other book had had some uncomfortable results, and it was evident to Butler that the literary critical method was not to be used with reference to Scripture: 'There are several ways of arguing which, though just with regard to other writings, are not applicable to scripture'. The Bible is not a book like other books. The Bible is like the world. It was with a sound sense of Butler's view of these matters that Southey selected for Butler's monument in Bristol a sentence from Origen's *Philocalia*:

He who believes the Scriptures to have proceeded from Him who is the Author of nature may well expect to find the same sort of difficulties in it as are found in the constitution of nature.

Butler was notoriously High Church. He was associated in the popular mind with stained glass and the crucifix. To him Scripture bore witness of a 'constitution of Nature' as cosmic liturgy. What Browne discerned of the human vocation in the Genesis announcement of *imago Dei*, Butler received from the witness in Hebrews to *sacerdos in aeternum*. Christ, 'the propitiatory sacrifice' for our sin, is, because he 'voluntarily offered up himself', to be acknowledged as 'our High Priest'. He is acknowledging us as sharers in his continuing liturgy. We are his 'holy brethren' in his 'sanctuary'. Butler tackles Tindal's satirical account of the Jews head on: 'The doctrine of this Epistle, then, plainly is that the legal sacrifices were allusions to the great and final atonement to be made by the blood of Christ'.

Browne had called a halt to theologizing at the moment when one might confuse the analogical with the univocal. He allowed that by divine analogy 'a plain vulgar word' might express 'Christ's mediation between God and Man', but he did not want to suggest that there was anything plain or vulgar in that mediation itself: 'the Real Nature and True Manner of Christ's intercession' for us is 'above Reason' and 'exempted from all our Enquiries'.[32] Browne became very angry with those who entertained the 'wild and extravagant' notion that the intercession of Christ is 'the very same in Nature of Kind with that which is human, but in super-excellent Degree'. Butler, however, took it that not only does theological language derive from vulgar talk of how things are with us, but that how things are here shows how they are in the Kingdom. They are always 'likely' to be 'like'. Butler says simply that God gave his Son for the help of the world 'in the same way of goodness' as God gives the assistance of neighbours to each one of us.

Butler could show with some forcefulness that what is happening in a scriptural narrative is 'in the same way' as what is happening in the life of a contemporary Christian. His recounting the story of Balaam instances this ability well.[33] Stillingfleet had taken the Numbers 22 story to be the original of what Lucian and Pausanias said of 'old Silenus': 'both noted for their skill in divination; both taken by water; both noted for riding on an ass'.[34] Tindal had made punning fun of 'a Number of Ideas' that the ass must have had 'to be able to reason with his master', and he had even greater pleasure in suggesting that whilst Peter reckoned the prophet mad, 'there does not appear anything like Madness' in the ass.[35] Butler brings the 'ass speaking with Man's voice' from the realms of folklore into the experience of his congregation. Whatever there is of madness in the story, Butler thinks it very like our ordinary experience. He took the Numbers story to be an account of 'a very wicked man' who yet lived 'under a deep sense of God'. Butler exclaimed, in mimicry of the decent Christian response to such a man, 'Good God, what inconsistency, what perplexity is here', but inconsistencies were his habitual study. 'Strange as it may appear', Balaam's condition is 'not altogether an uncommon one'. Butler has looked about him and, 'with some small alterations' and 'put a little lower', he has seen such a person often enough: 'For if the reasonable choice be seen and acknowledged, and yet men make the unreasonable one, is not this the same contradiction, that very inconsistency which appeared so unaccountable?' As Balaam's attitude is to right reasoning, just so, though perhaps 'put a little lower', is the attitude of the eighteenth-century man sitting beneath Butler's pulpit.[36]

But Butler's derivation of good things from the story comes to a sudden stop at the ass. The delight of the talking ass and the angry angel, the fun of Balaam's pronouncing a blessing when he intended a curse, the repeated mockery of the Moabites as they climb hills, build altars and offer animals, does not escape Butler. He is aware of the story-telling techniques being employed by the 'sacred historian' who writes of seven altars, seven oxen and seven rams, 'in order to engage the reader's attention'. But he cannot discern how these elements of the story-telling, in the very process of the story's being told, further the author's theological intention.

The story is, he saw, deliberately unlikely. But it is through the unlikelihood of the talking ass that the action of the story is advanced and the meaning of the story declared. The talking ass communicates the meaning of those incidents, making them understandable to those who are in positions analogous to that of the inconsistent prophet. The ass announces what present readers are to receive as divine meaning. Butler found himself unable, for reasons of temperament, to go forward with the unlikely narrative, and unable, for reasons of theological integrity, to go against the narrative. He remained uneasily in the 'analogical' whilst puzzling at this demand to go beyond the 'probable'. He let the story slip.

Butler was generally thought, quite mistakenly, to have answered the deist theses conclusively. He had simply countered the deist description of the world with a description of his own. He knew he had not proved much: 'The fore-going treatise is not satisfactory, very far indeed from it'. But he had put together assumptions about an Eternal God, an immortal soul, and the kind of world that we inhabit, which enabled contemporary Christians to move forward from the ante-diluvian sticking-place of Browne's *imago Dei*. And, in his recognition of the pain and fear and maddening strangeness of our lives, Butler proved himself more adventuresome and more compassionate than those who were content to leave things as they were in a post-diluvian world. Viscount Bolingbroke (1678–1751) asserted that 'Whatever is, is best'. Butler was anxious to change the conditions in which too many human beings have to live. He was anxious to change human beings themselves. Whatever is, is ready for conversion.

That conversion occurs when human beings, in accord with their true nature, are living within that 'progressive state' of 'the glorious liberty of the children of God'. Butler's enthusiasm is not simply for life: it is for liberated life.

During the deist debates, individual controversialists had declared that they had specific liberties in view. Toland had delighted to 'live in a free government', and had contrasted his good state with that of those' who at no extraordinary distance from us groan under the yoke of absolute dominion'; but he wanted 'Gypsies, Vagabonds, and Beggarly Strangers' to be 'taken up and severely handled'. He had written, too, a tract supporting the Elector Jan Wellems in his persecution of Protestants in the Palatinate. And, confident in 'the enjoyment of Christian Liberty', he proposed to release 'the Slaves of the Levitical and Pagan Priesthoods', directing his mission especially to those who were captive to the 'Jewish Rabbies' and 'their mad Liberty of Allegory'.[37] King, in his consideration of 'the pleasure of choosing', had been 'very Sensible that great Contentions and Divisions have happened in the Church about Predestination', but he had not thought it his business to note what social, economic or political difficulties might be in the way of his fellows' exercise of choice.[38] Tindal, 'defending the Liberties given by God to Mankind', was eager to assert that 'he leaves Men at Liberty in all Things indifferent', but he could not work out how men's appointing among themselves 'Time, Place, Persons, and all other Things which require special Determination' should be freely managed.[39] He could only guess at the restriction of choice arising from varieties of reasoning power, cultural condition and experience. Browne, characteristically announcing that 'this is not the proper Place to enlarge upon human liberty', goes on, equally characteristically, to review and attack 'many erroneous Opinions' about human freedom. But at the end he is not really interested in the topic, declaring himself contented that whatever we mean by 'this Liberty' should be 'transferred to God by Analogy'.[40]

Butler is more humane. His mind is larger. He collects every sense of 'liberty' into his meditation upon that *'perfect love* which St John speaks of', which, 'as it implies an entire coincidence of our wills with the will of God', must be 'a state of absolute freedom in the most literal and proper sense'.[41]

St John further speaks of the wind that 'bloweth where it listeth', and in a sermon on that text Butler suggests that we may 'fairly infer the freedom of God's grace'. All our liberties have their origin in God's own freedom. 'He giveth it liberally.' And he gives in a large range of circumstance. 'Every admonition from the pulpit, every wholesome law, every advice from a friend, or a parent, every good book, every pious example, every motion and intention to do well, every check of conscience, is a blowing of this wind.'[42] Nothing in British theology comes nearer the tone of 'I have I know not what within my heart' than Butler's hesitant description of the delicate influence of the Spirit who moves us 'without our having any distinct perception of the thing'. The gracious effect is 'visible' but 'the manner of it imperceptible'. It was, indeed, as he told Wesley, 'a horrid thing, a very horrid thing' to make a claim to recognize the manner of the Spirit at work.[43] Butler's sense of the divine origin of our freedom prevents his making any division between political, physical and moral liberty. Those who live under a despot, those who are kept prisoner, and those who are caught in sin, are each of them deprived of a share in the one liberty effected by the Spirit of God.

His 'admonition from the pulpit' commonly originates in the examination of 'wholesome law'. Butler rejoices in the 'security of our liberty' provided by the British constitution.[44] 'In some other countries the upper part of the world is free, but in Great Britain the whole body of the people is free.' He is loyal to a king who secures a free people 'from that Pretender to his crown' who would abrogate those constitutional liberties. And, at the same time, he is keen that 'the spirit of liberty' should be kept up by legal, regular opposition to the king's government. From political liberty, he derives economic and social liberties. Butler took immense satisfaction in Parliament's having 'emancipated our northern provinces from most of their legal remains of slavery' by passing in 1747 a bill to guarantee 'a reasonable wage' to miners.[45] The responsibilities of the governors of Britain for the governed did not, however, cease on the establishment of political and economic liberty. 'More particular regard should be had to the education of the lower people here, than in places where they are born slaves of power', for here they are more likely to become 'slaves of superstition'.[46]

If we realize that we must secure the liberty of the Durham miners, and see that their children have free access to the emancipating powers of education, we must also realize that we have 'an obligation but little more remote' to secure the Christian liberty of those enslaved in 'our factories abroad'.[47] Butler, in meditating the reference of 'perfect love' and 'absolute freedom', took a long look at the colonial system.

Toland had not thought about 'such an Island as Jamaica' or 'the Discovery of America' except as diversions in a dullish discussion of 'Matters of Fact'. He only entertained the idea of a mission in order to declare that if he 'would go to preach to the Wild Indians' he would very quickly settle whatever argument they had about the uses of language.[48] In much the same vein, King had been content to employ 'an ignorant American' as an example in an argument for the usefulness of writing.[49] Butler interested himself in both the political government and the theological education of the Americans. 'Free government supposes that the conduct of affairs may be inquired into', he told the House of Lords, 'and spoken of with freedom.'[50] He spoke of the government that the colonists exercised over the Indians and the Negroes. He knew, without any delaying in comparative religion studies, what he should say about the Indians. We have entered into a relation of 'neighbourhood' with them through 'our having gotten possessions in their country'. Butler's appreciation of the mediation of Christ for the race demanded that we assist them as neighbours 'in the same way of goodness' as God is assisting us. The Indians are 'one family with ourselves, the family of mankind'. We must, therefore, 'instruct them in our common salvation'. The analogy of religion and nature, all that earlier talk of the chrysalis coming into new powers as a butterfly, gave him the language in which to talk of a 'capacity' in the Indians corresponding to a vital power in revelation which should enable them to enjoy 'an higher state of life hereafter'.[51]

He knew, too, what he should say of the Negroes. They also are 'of the race of mankind for whom Christ died', and they too have a 'capacity' to enjoy the order revealed in Hebrews. But he found that his analogical language failed him as he spoke of colonial government. Horrified that the slaves 'are for our advantage made as miserable as they well can be', he does not have unworthy recourse to justifications of the system. He admits that he has been brought up against a reality which cannot be extended towards the Kingdom.[52] Slavery is impatient of analogy. There are no probabilities of 'likeness' in the institution; and nothing in Scripture to help him make sense of the slaves' condition.

It is a signal witness to the honesty of Butler's mind at this point that he simply abandoned his habitual theological instruments. He makes a desperate appeal to the governors to acknowledge that 'obligation of charity' to connect 'suffering' with 'salvation', and through their misery 'in the present world' to put the slaves 'into as advantageous a situation as we are able with regard to another'. Those who are, under British rule, slaves of power must be brought out of the slavery of superstition in readiness for that perfect love. They must be shown the liturgical order in their own place. He proposed that bishoprics be set up in the colonies as a pledge of the Church's intent to work among them for the establishment of the order derived from Hebrews. He has, in considering the demand for 'liberty' that the humanity of the slaves makes upon him, given up every claim for the 'logical' consistency of his 'analogy'.

Yet he remained quite incapable of telling his congregations a story of that Kingdom in which all should enjoy a mutual liberty. He could not even tell himself a story in which he should be free.

When Butler lay on his deathbed, he confessed to his chaplain that 'though I have endeavoured to avoid sin and to please God to the utmost of my power, yet, from the consciousness of perpetual infirmities, I am still afraid to die'. The analogy of rewards hereafter would only have worked at such a moment if Butler had felt that virtue was in some way rewarded here, and he did not often feel that. The affirmation of a coming completion in virtuous well-being could only be made if Butler were conscious of some progressive command of his infirmities. He did not feel that either. Like the slave, he needed the surprise of reversal. It was given him. He was to cease thinking of his avoidance of sin, his anxious endeavours and his perpetual infirmities. 'My Lord', said his graceful chaplain, 'it is written, Him that cometh to me, I will in no wise cast out.' The figure of the welcoming Lord is a figure of imaginative power. 'True', replied the dying man, 'and I am surprised that though I have read that Scripture a thousand times over, I never felt its virtue till this moment, and now I die happy.'[53]

His proposal for an episcopal order in the American colonies came to nothing. The Act protecting the miners of his County Palatine was repealed. In a charge to the clergy of his Durham diocese, Butler had paused to contemplate the ways in which the ancient Greeks had made their divinities 'the chief subject of statuary, sculpture, painting, and poetry'. He observed similar expressions of religion in contemporary travellers' accounts of the heathen; and he knew about such things among the Roman Catholics. Butler fumbled for a moment in search of some way of translating this service of imagination that would be appropriate in Georgian devotion. But he could not find it. His sermon on Balaam, recoiling from story and from every exercise of imagination, remained a concise paradigm of the way theology was to be done in England.

It is a great loss that Handel did not attempt the story of Balaam and his ass. Handel's extraordinary talent for imitative music would have prompted a deliciously funny and exactly asinine music. But he did, in a splendid series of works of the imagination, explore how mythical, political and social representations of liberty were related to that liberation which is expressed in scriptural story.

Notes

1 E. Stillingfleet, *Origines Sacrae, or a Rational Account of the Grounds of Natural and Revealed Religion* (1662); quotations from Book III, pp. 138–57.

2 Cf. L. Stephen, *English Thought in the Eighteenth Century* (1876) I, p. 102.

3 R. E. Sullivan, *John Toland and the Deist Controversy* (Harvard, 1982), p. 19.

4 Cf. Pierre Des Maizeaux (ed.), *Collection of Several Pieces of Mr John Toland* (2 vols; 1726), biographical introduction.

5 Cf. E. Stillingfleet, *Vindication of the Doctrine of the Trinity* (1697) and Stephen, *op. cit.*, p. 111.

6 Stephen Nye, *Agreement of the Unitarians with the Catholic Church* (1697), p. 55.

7 J. Toland, *Christianity not Mysterious, or a Treatise shewing That there is nothing in the Gospel Contrary to Reason, Nor Above it* (1696); quotations from pp. 4–6, 24, 49–52, 119 and 147–54.

8 R. Blome, *Present State of His Majestie's Isles and Territories in America* (1687), pp. 205, 212, 241.

9 W. Bosman, *New and Accurate Description of the Coast of Guinea* (1704), Eng. trans. (1705), pp. 147–54.

10 J. Toland, *Letters to Serena* (1704) III, paras 1 and 3.

11 M. de la Créquinière, *Conformité des coutumes des Indiens orientaux avec des autres peuples de l'antiquité* (1704), trans. J. Toland (1705), p. 27.

12 W. King, *Divine Predestination and Fore-knowledge Consistent with the Freedom of Man's Will* (Dublin, 1709), pp. 7–13.

13 10 September 1720; quoted from King's papers at Trinity College, Dublin, in Sullivan, *op. cit.*, p. 39.

14 C. Burney, 'Sketch of the life of Handel' in *An Account of the Musical*

Performances in Westminster Abbey and the Pantheon (1785); cited by W. Dean and J. M. Knapp, *Handel's Operas, 1704–1726* (1987), p. 494.

15 Cf. B. Feldman and R. D. Richardson, *Rise of Modern Mythology, 1680–1860* (Indiana, 1972), p. 42.

16 J. Lafiteau, *Moeurs des sauvages Amériquains comparées aux moeurs des premiers temps* (1724); excerpts trans. Feldman and Richardson, *op. cit.*, pp. 47–9.

17 A. de' Liguori, *De Incarnazione*, Discourse IX, 2, trans. E. Grimm (Cincinnati, 1886), p. 133.

18 E. Stillingfleet, *Origines Sacrae* II, p. 155.

19 Cf. D. C. Allen, 'Milton and the descent to light', *Journal of English and German Philology* 60 (1961), pp. 614–30; M. Y. Hughes, 'The Arthurs of the *Faerie Queene*', *Études anglaises* 6 (1953), pp. 193–213; F. M. Krouse, *Milton's Samson and the Christian Tradition* (New York, 1974), pp. 73ff.

20 A. Ramsay, *The Travels of Cyrus*, 'to which is annex'd a discourse upon the theology and mythology of the ancients' (1727), pp. 81–4, 116 and 126.

21 Isaac Reed (ed.), *Biographia Dramatica* (1782) II, p. 315.

22 Cf. W. Wollaston, *Religion of Nature Delineated* (1722), p. 202.

23 Cf. M. Tindal, *Christianity as old as the Creation, or, The Gospel a republication of the Religion of Nature* I (1730), p. 317; following quotations from pp. 8, 101, 342, 404, 31, 385ff. and 152.

24 W. Law, *The Case of Reason*, in *Works* (1762) II, pp. 7 and 28.

25 P. Browne, *A Letter in Answer to a Book called Christianity not Mysterious* (1697).

26 P. Browne, *Things Divine and Supernatural* (1733), p. 260; further quotations from pp. 42–3, 49, 457–8.

27 Cf. J. Tucker, *Humble Address and earnest Appeal to the Landed Interest* (1755), p. 20.

28 Leonard Huxley (ed.), *Life and Letters of T. H. Huxley* (2 vols; 1900) I, p. 259.

29 Toland, *Christianity not Mysterious*, pp. 12–13, 19.

30 Tindal, *Christianity as Old as the Creation*, p. 183.

31 J. Butler, *Works*, ed. W. E. Gladstone (2 vols; 1896), *Analogy*, Introduction; further quotations from Part I, ch. 1, paras 1, 2, 27 and 30; Part II, ch. 3, para. 12, and ch. 5, paras 13 and 17.

32 P. Browne, *Things Divine*, p. 529.

33 Butler, *ed. cit.*, *XV Sermons*, vii.

34 Stillingfleet, *Origines Sacrae* II, p. 157.

35 Tindal, *Christianity as Old as the Creation*, pp. 54–5.

36 Butler, *ed. cit.*, *VI Sermons*, iii, 3.

37 J. Toland, *Art of Governing* (1701), p. 3; Pierre Des Maizeaux (ed.), *Memorial Presented to a Minister of State* II (1726), pp. 255-6; *Declaration Lately Published by the Elector Palatine* (1707); *Christianity not Mysterious*, pp. xxi and 55.

38 W. King, *Divine Predestination*, p. 37.

39 Tindal, *Christianity as Old as the Creation*, pp. 121-2.

40 Browne, P., *Things Divine*, p. 313.

41 Butler, *ed. cit.*, *VI Sermons*, iii, 3.

42 This sermon is attributed to Butler by Bartlett (see note 53 below) and reprinted in Butler, *ed. cit.*, pp. 441-6.

43 Cf. Butler, *ed. cit.* II, pp. 434-5.

44 Butler, *ed. cit.*, *VI Sermons*, iii, 13.

45 *Ibid.*, v, 5, 12-14 and 6.

46 *Ibid.*, ii, 18.

47 *Ibid.*, i, 11.

48 Toland, *Christianity not Mysterious*, pp. 40 and 28-9.

49 King, *Divine Predestination*, p. 16.

50 Butler, *ed. cit.*, *VI Sermons*, iii, 25.

51 *Ibid.*, i, 13.

52 *Ibid.*, i, 12.

53 Cf. Thomas Bartlett, *Memoirs of Bishop Butler* (1839).

3

A revaluation of narrative

SCRIPTURE AND MYTH, 1739–45

During 1735 and 1736 the opera company's finances tottered towards ruin. The 1736 season opened with a revival of *Alcina*, there was a gala performance of *Atalanta* for the Prince of Wales's birthday, and, after some delays, Handel produced his new opera, *Arminio*, in January 1737. This unhappy piece was based on an old libretto by Salvi, an acquaintance of Handel's Florence days, and was wholly lacking in appeal to contemporary taste. But at least it got performed. His next opera, *Giustino*, was cancelled by a sudden and wholly unprecedented ban on opera performances during Lent that year. Handel revived his oratorio repertory. *Il Trionfo del Tempo* came out again, so did *Esther*, so did the *Athalia* music as *Il Parnasso in Festa*. But it surprised his friends that he could not make more out of his rivals' discomfort and compose a new oratorio that would entirely vindicate him as the master of London music. Handel it seemed had lost the will to compose. To pay his wages bill, he had had to draw out almost the whole of his savings, and Mainwaring recorded that in this period 'the observation that misfortunes rarely come single, was verified in Handel', for 'his fortune was not more impaired than his health and his understanding'. Handel had a stroke which left his right arm paralysed. And he suffered a most frightening derangement of his mind: 'How greatly his senses were distorted at intervals', Mainwaring delicately observed, 'appeared from a hundred instances, which are better forgotten'.

Handel had tried the waters of Tunbridge Wells twice before. This time he went to Aachen, where, in his impatience to be well, he sat in the vapour baths 'near three times as long as hath ever been the practice'. The stratagem worked: 'The use of his fingers was restor'd to him; his Spirits grew Calm'. On the collapse of the Opera of the Nobility, plans were made for him to set up again with 'Count' John Jacob Heidegger (1666–1749), the Swiss impresario at the King's Theatre in the Haymarket, and he hurried back to London to begin work on yet another romantic *opera seria*, *Faramondo*, in mid-November. On 20 November, Queen Caroline died. The court went into mourning. The theatres shut.

The anthem 'The ways of Zion do mourn' that Handel composed for the funeral in mid-December is the only work of Handel that Butler is for a certainty known to have heard. As Clerk of the Closet, he walked in the procession and had a place in the service. This time the Dean of Westminster chose the texts. Extracts from the Psalms, Lamentations, Job, and the Pauline epistles were arranged in an intelligent order. Handel evidently appreciated their coherent sense. His anthem is an elegy of appropriate sensibility. The German Queen was interred to music that hinted broadly of the Lutheran chorale. But there were as many pointers to the future as delicate references to the past. It is at once apparent that the attempts Handel had made at writing German church music and continued in his successful management of the Roman liturgical style, here culminate in so perfect a realization of the English religious tone that he must be encouraged to do more in this way. And immediately the listener is apprised that the shift of the balance of *opera seria* from solo to chorus, which was being worked out in *Athalia*, is completed in the Anthem. It is an entirely choral work. Handel's ingenuity in varying the effect must have been a delightful revelation of his own gifts as he composed.

Events were conspiring to push Handel into renewing his oratorio writing. *Faramondo* just about paid its way; *Serse*, its successor, did not — despite the presence in the first scene of 'Handel's *Largo*', and despite, or perhaps because of, some wry touches of humour amidst the *opera seria* conventions. When Heidegger tried to raise a subscription for the next season there were so few takers that he had to abandon the scheme on 25 July. Handel had been warned of the cancellation. On 23 July 1738 he had already taken up a text that had been waiting for a time when he might 'read it with all the Attention it deserves'. It had waited several years. During the summer of 1738 he worked on Charles Jennens' text of *Saul*.

The madman in the mad world: *Saul* (1739)

It had been part of Butler's perplexity as he applied to Josiah Tucker for assistance in considering the origins of madness, that 'as to divines we have no data, either from Scripture, or from reason, to go upon, relative to this affair'. But it is precisely with the onset of madness that Handel is concerned when he makes his first attempt to retell a scriptural story, and to do so in a way that will demonstrate something of the freedom of the self.

It is not unnatural that, after the derangement of his own mind, Handel should be meditating upon madness. It is entirely in accord with the direction of his meditations that he should now explore this terror through the retelling of a biblical narrative. It is immensely striking, however, that the man who had himself been under the shadow of insanity should, in his account of the madness of an Israelite king, have so great an interest in the ways in which an individual's madness may affect the lives of those around him. *Saul* is concerned not only with Saul, but with Saul amongst his family, his retainers and his nation.

It would be possible to make even the hectic story of Saul into a reverent meditation on the facts of living. The librettist of J.C. Schieferdecker's *Der königliche Prophete David* (c. 1700) had done so, allegorizing the love of David for Jonathan into the love of Christ for the soul.[1] But Jennens was a lively-minded person, not to be caught in such dullness. An eccentric and prayerful Non-Juror, rich from the inherited profits of Birmingham foundries, engagingly extravagant, generous to the poor, friendly to the dissenter, Jennens possessed a fine sense of dramatic structure. Handel acknowledged this when he reverted to Jennens' scheme for *Saul* after trying out some notions of his own.

Jennens' *Saul* was divided into three acts. He provided stage directions not for manager or actor but for the composer, enabling Handel the better to envisage the oratorio's action on the stage of the mind. Act I begins with an 'Epinicon', an Israelite song of triumph at the defeat of Goliath. This ushers in the young David. At once the clash of interests is sounded in Saul's court. Jonathan, the king's son, seeks the intimate friendship of the valiant hero; his sister Michal falls at once in love with the handsome young man; and his elder sister Merab reacts with a rather British snobbery towards the peasant farmer's boy. Ironically, it is to Merab that Saul engages David. After an orchestral 'symphony', it is Saul's turn to react to the up-and-coming man when the Israelite women sing the famously undiplomatic chorus:

Saul who hast thy thousands slain
Welcome to thy friends again!

David his ten thousands slew,
Ten thousand praises are his due.

Saul's reaction is to shift from political unease, 'What can they give him more, except the Kingdom?', to personal jealousy and murderous sullenness. Michal thinks to calm her father by getting David to play his harp. But the king feels baited beyond endurance and hurls his javelin at the musician. As David runs from his presence, Saul orders Jonathan to kill his friend. In Act II, Jonathan, having told David not only of Saul's threat but of the breaking of his engagement to Merab, manages to patch up something that looks like peace between Saul and David; the king even bestows the loving Michal on David. But when, against Saul's expectations, David returns victorious again from the battle with the Philistines, the javelin whizzes through the air. By this time all three of Saul's children are appalled at his increasingly insane pursuit of David. The people, too, begin to understand that Saul is stepping towards his own destruction.

'Wretch that I am! of my own ruin author.' Saul knows as well as any of them what he is doing to himself. But he does not feel free to stop himself. Like Macbeth, he thinks that 'Things bad begun make strong themselves by ill'. Like Macbeth, he seeks out a witch to tell him the future. He demands that she show him the great spirit of Samuel. The ghost traces Saul's present misfortune back to the moment when, for the sake of a ransom, Saul spared the enemy of God, Agag the king of the Amalekites. For this hidden cause, victory and the kingdom will be given to David. Another symphony portrays the battle. Then a messenger tells David of the death of Jonathan in the thick of the fight, and of Saul, who has botched his suicide, asking the messenger to finish him off. 'Who are you?', asks David. 'I am an Amalekite.' In a perfect reversal of the Agag incident, demonstrating that he is truly God's champion, David orders the death of the heathen who had dared to touch the Lord's anointed. 'Impious wretch, of race accurst.' Thereupon the Dead March is played for the funeral procession of Saul and Jonathan.

If it would be a miscategorization to make a claim for Jennens as a dramatist, for his text would never stand up by itself, it is clear that he is, with da Ponte, Boito, Wagner and Peter Gabriel, one of the very few great wordsmiths in the history of European music. He has an extraordinary sensitivity in the making of verses for a composer. And he is remarkably sure of the direction in which Handel should go after

Athalia. Humphreys had thrust the action of that oratorio into a Platonical, cyclic scheme, leaving Handel to make what he could of the biblical characters. Jennens gives Handel every chance of creating a Greek hero within the framework of a biblical narrative. Scripture, Jennens maintains through *Saul*, does offer an explanation for the occurrence of madness. If Saul does not understand why all these things are happening to him, still the ransoming of Agag is not precisely like the murder of Laius by Oedipus. Saul knew precisely what crime he was committing; he just thought he could get away with it. He had opportunity and freedom for choice as he stepped towards madness. Jennens is very skilful in maintaining through the oratorio both the classical structure of 'fatal flaw' in the king's character and the biblical affirmation of personal responsibility.

Handel was not so confident that the categories of Greek flaw or, as Jennens understood it, of Hebrew sin, would adequately account for the terror within *Saul*. He proves, when confronted by the simple nexus between Agag and the witch of Endor, as hesitant as Butler. He will not insist on a relation between some easily identifiable incidence of disobedience and the loss of rational self-control. If, in the *Analogy*, Butler had allowed that miseries follow upon imprudence and wilfulness and vice, he had insisted that they follow disguisedly: 'For instance, sickness and untimely death is a consequence of intemperance though accompanied with the highest mirth and jollity'. And he had pointed out that 'we cannot find by experience that all our sufferings are owing to our follies'. We do not easily recognize a connection between 'storms and tempests, earthquakes, famine, pestilence' and our vices.[2] And, most puzzlingly always for him, we know nothing of a moral law by which insanity comes on human beings. Handel was more of his opinion than of Jennens'. Offered a chorus whose general tone is indicated by its opening verse:

> What words can tell how happy they
> Who all their God's commands obey!

he first hoped to alter its effect by placing his musical emphasis on an image of the sea

> Whose waves tumultuous roar
> And tossing mire and dirt affront the shoar,

which was rather nearer to his own sense of the unbiddable force crashing in the mind of the madman, but then decided it would be better to give up all attempt at setting such lines.

The autograph of *Saul* makes it immediately clear that the composition of this oratorio entailed a great struggle for Handel. He was continually crossing out what he had written, rewriting, crossing out again, rewriting again. He was discovering new forces of musical imagination, new capacities of realizing patterns of emotion, as he tried to express the terrifying collapse of mental and social liberty in Saul and Saul's society. Handel's imaginative reach into unheard-of places demanded unheard-of instruments: the carillon which sounded like 'some squirrels in a cage' and, equally reverberating with the deprivation of liberty, 'the largest kettle drums in the Tower'. His determination to bring the fearsome realities of madness within his musical compass was signified when he ordered a new organ from whose commanding bench he might control the vast orchestral noise. Handel was not going to allow his audience to think that there was some usual explanation for all that was happening in *Saul*. They were to feel the strangeness of the world.

Looking for Zoroastro

The perplexed heroes of *Orlando* and *Alcina* had, like Wollaston, recognized their need of a guide among the perplexities of experience. After *Saul*'s declaration of those perplexities, Handel hoped that his audience would acknowledge their own need of such a guide and, like Wollaston, identify the scriptural revelation as the guide for them.

Neither Orlando nor Ruggiero had needed to be told how to conduct themselves properly in situations of ordinary living. They had called to Zoroastro and Melisso precisely because the world was not as it had been described to them. Handel did not want to propose scriptural revelation as a reasonable guide to decent behaviour. He intended his next oratorios to persuade his audience that the scriptural narratives were appropriate to the experience of that strangeness he had been announcing in *Saul*. He was to discover that it was no easy thing to identify the sort of oratorio that would fulfil this function. And, equally, no easy matter to identify just what sort of guidance the scriptural narratives were actually offering. It was only through the interacting exploration of oratorio form and scriptural witness, sustained in a lengthy series of works, that Handel arrived at his understanding of either. From *Saul* he went on to the significant failure of *Israel in Egypt*.

Israel in Egypt (1739)
Handel seems this time to have chosen the texts himself, lifting them

almost unaltered from the 'Song of Moses' in Exodus 15. He was not planning any great enterprise, just hoping to keep himself financially afloat and mentally busy whilst the question of biblical oratorio settled itself in his mind. The thing grew as he struggled to get it into shape. In his final version, the 'Song of Moses' came to be preceded by a setting of the plagues that descended on the Egyptians when they refused to let God's people go. These plagues were themselves now prefaced by a solemn music bringing to mind, he hoped, the collapse of Israelite life in Egypt on the death of Joseph. *Israel in Egypt* was thus constructed from a choral anthem, a supplementary set of choruses intended to fit what had already been composed, and introductory music originally used in Queen Caroline's funeral anthem. The oratorio which resulted had, quite naturally, an anthematic rather than a dramatic identity. More than any other of his works, it fits the 'church-going mood' of performance.

'Exodus', which is now Part I of *Israel in Egypt*, begins with the tenor announcement of the time and place of the action: 'there arose a new king over Egypt'; then the chorus tells us the appropriate response to this news: 'the children of Israel sigh'd'. The work is largely held together by a sequence of such choral reaction to solo announcements. The linking recitative has rather the effect of the exhortatory narrative by the evangelist in the Passion liturgy in German churches. It is meant to persuade; and so are the moments of imitative and illustrative cleverness in the plague music. 'Thick darkness' is to come upon the ear as a disturbing presence, we are to be among people who are groping their way, unable to find each other, each part hearing the others as if in distant alleys of a city. Handel, with fine Lutheran orthodoxy, is challenging the merit-conscious bourgeois to see themselves as lost, as finding their way only by the guiding will of God, knowing that they are saved only in faith. At this moment, at least, it is possible to accept Bloch's judgement that in Handel's oratorios 'music resounded with the best in the soul of Luther and his fellow spirits', though Handel is not yet in *Israel in Egypt* expressing 'the great Judaeo-heroic streak which created the whole Reformation movement'.[3] But the listener is unlikely to respond in the way that Handel intends, and not simply from some unregenerate clinging to good works and their merit before God.

The failure of *Israel in Egypt* is a failure to demonstrate that what is going on in the music has any vital connection with what is going on in life. The work retains its character as anthem. It is music to which a congregation might listen. Sung by others. About others. When, at the end, the soprano repeats the opening line of the 'Song of Moses', the circle of music-makers is complete. Those who are not singing or playing this music are shut out. *Israel in Egypt* is as liturgically distancing as the Latin Vespers of Cardinal Colonna's Carmelites to which, as one of their clients noted sadly, so few Romans came. Yet the reviewer for the *London Daily Post* wrote of 'the noblest Adoration and Homage paid to the Deity' and associated *Israel in Egypt* with 'Protestant, free, virtuous, united Christian England', against 'slavish, bigotted, disunited, unchristian Popery'. The oratorio was a box-office flop: Handel would have to work harder if others were to appreciate the kind of freedom he was finding in the scriptural texts.

The thought of how much effort would be required for such a project seems for a while to have daunted Handel. Lord Egmont, in his diary for 8 April 1741, reported that Handel was going off for another dip in the German baths. There was a rumour that the performance that night would be 'probably his last for ever in this Country'. He may, that summer, have thought of retiring. In July, Jennens reported that he was not going to compose anything that winter. But Handel came bustling back in mid-August. The liveliness of the oracles of God was to be manifest in *Messiah*.

Messiah (1742)

There has been some debate whether Jennens may not have taken the rather churchy course of culling texts from the Prayer Book to make what Handel graciously termed 'your *Messiah*'. He could have found the passages used for Part I in the Christmas service, and most of those for Part III in the burial service, and the Part II texts all occur at notable moments of the liturgical calendar. But Jennens, however prompted by memories of these ecclesial contexts, may just as well have found for himself those places in the Old and New Testaments which Christians had traditionally used in their accounts of the coming, the redemptive life and death of Jesus, and their own share in the wonder of resurrection. All these texts were part of the common conversation in the culture within which Jennens and Handel had been brought up.

Indeed most of these texts had very recently been fought over in a debate about 'prophecy' between orthodox and deist. Jennens' choice of scriptural passages for *Messiah* is a deliberate attempt to reconstitute that account of 'salvation history' which Humphreys had equally deliberately removed from Racine's *Athalie*. The librettist was enabling the composer to make a statement in favour of Establishment theory. The way that such a debate would go was hinted at in Toland's ridicule of those who thought to 'find all the New Testament in the Old' and the response made in the 1707 Boyle Lectures of William Whiston (1667–1752) on *The Accomplishment of Scripture Prophecies*. But it had really only got going with the publication by Anthony Collins (1676–1729) of *The Grounds and Reasons of the Christian Religion* in 1724. By the time Collins produced his *Literal Scheme of Prophecy* in 1726, 35 treatises on the topic had been published in England. Jennens' textual catena for *Messiah* has to be read as a late but not conclusive contribution to the orthodox apologetic being carried on in such polemical tracts as the *Practical Discourses on the Principal Representations of the Messiah through the Old Testament* by William Harris in 1724, *The Use and Intent of Prophecy* by one of Queen Caroline's protégés, 'the plunging prelate' Thomas Sherlock, in 1725, Samuel Clarke's *Discourse concerning the Connexion of the Prophecies in the Old Testament and the Application of them to Christ*, of the same year, and *A Demonstration of the Messias* by Richard Kidder in 1726. Tindal had had some destructive fun in pointing to texts 'which, if taken literally, look as tho' the Prophets were either deceiv'd themselves, or were willing to deceive others'. He cut off a discussion of the relevance of such texts to Christology with the modest acknowledgement that 'I must, as to the Prophecies in the Old Testament, confess my Ignorance, that I do not understand them'.[4] This controversy still echoes, in very much the same language of dismissal and outrage at dismissal, in Thomas Newton's *Dissertations on the Prophecies* of 1754. *Messiah* stands in the middle of a debate whose beginning is very like its end.

Handel knew that Jennens was making a statement in this controversy. He knew that in accepting Jennens' texts for such a 'sacred oratorio' he was making his own affirmation that the Old Testament was prophetic of Jesus. *Messiah* represents, in this context, the adoption of a theological programme. The Pentateuch, the histories of Israel, the prophetic books, even, as Handel showed by *Susanna*, the deuterocanonical literature, as they are set out in his oratorios, were to be understood as leading towards the revelation of God in Christ.

Jennens understood very well the delicate character of this enterprise. He recognized that putting scriptural texts to music, especially texts which had in the last twenty years become laden with peculiar controversial interests, might offend many of those who constituted their expected audience. Everyone was nervous of New Testament words being further reduced in authority by being sung in a theatre by singers of doubtful reputation among decent folk. So it is understandable that Jennens could not approve the speed with which

Handel polished off their oratorio. He thought the dignity of the scriptural passages should have commanded at least a full year's attention from the composer. He suggested, in July 1741, that Handel take until the autumn to prepare his thoughts for *Messiah*, write the music during the winter months, and perform the oratorio during Holy Week 1742. Jennens did not at all care for Handel's carrying off *Messiah*, having finished it in November, for performance in Dublin, without any word to him: 'I shall put no more Sacred Works into his hands, to be thus abus'd'. It took him some time to recover his balance. In 1743 he was still trying to get Handel to retouch *Messiah* 'to make it fit for publick performance' in London, and finding Handel 'so lazy and so obstinate' that he could get nothing changed.

It was the question of the biblical text that 'Philalethes' most famously addressed in a letter to the *Universal Spectator* of 19 March 1743, in anticipation of that first London performance about which Jennens was getting so fussed. *Israel in Egypt* had been offensive enough in its quotations from the scriptural text, 'but it seems that the Old Testament is not to be prophan'd alone, nor God by the name of Jehovah only, but the New must be join'd with it, and God by the most sacred and merciful name of Messiah'. Handel's manager at Covent Garden may have been hoping to avoid the thrust of this objection when he advertised not '*Messiah*' but 'A New Sacred Oratorio'. But 'Philalethes' had hit on Handel's intention. It was important to Handel that the text should be appreciated as a sacred text, and that it should be plainly heard and comprehended. He was not now writing music to disguise a doggerel Italian libretto which few in his audience would understand.

There is an indication of Handel's concern for clarity and communicativeness in his choice of the contralto for the first performances in Dublin. The part had been carefully fitted to the voice of Susanna Maria Cibber, which, Burney says, was 'a thread', and her musicality, 'whereof', says Sheridan, she had 'but a very moderate share'. What Handel found precisely to his purpose was her 'intelligence of the words', her 'native feeling', her 'powers of expression'. As the poet of 'To Mrs Cibber' had it in the *Gentleman's Magazine* of March 1742:

> O wondrous girl! how small a space
> Includes the gift of human race!

Mrs Cibber was later the greatest actress of her day, and the constant partner of David Garrick in the classical repertory. She was the singer to make an audience attend to the words, learn what Handel was intending them to feel, share what he was suggesting they should know about themselves as 'human race'. She bore the central line of meaning that Handel discerned in Jennens' collection of texts. He gave her several of the best tunes so that the most significant verses should be impressed upon the minds and hearts of his hearers: the prophecy of a liberator in 'Behold! a virgin shall conceive', the effectiveness of liberation in 'Then shall the eyes of the blind be open'd', and, most movingly, the cost of liberty, 'He was despised and rejected of men'. The old Halle Pietist belief in a peculiar urgency of divine inspiration at specific points in the biblical text is given vital expression in Handel's setting of these words. And Mrs Cibber achieved just that immediacy of meaning for which Handel had been working: 'The whole audience solemnly rose up in joint acknowledgement that He who for our sakes "had been despised and rejected of men" was their Creator, Redeemer, King of Kings, Lord of Lords'.

The objections 'Philalethes' was making were not to be satisfied by such general enthusiasm:

> Are the most sacred Things, Religion and the Holy Bible, which is the Word of God, to be prostituted to the perverse Humour of a Set of obstinate People, on a Supposition that they may be forc'd thereby once in their Lives to attend to what is serious?

He put the logical poser: 'an Oratorio either is an Act of Religion, or it is not'. He meant to set people thinking about whether a company of players were 'fit Ministers of God's Word'. They were not to set such a question aside by some specious suggestion that there would be an occasion of piety in the performance for those who did not generally go to church. 'Philalethes', like the rest of those who attempted to contribute to this and similar debates, puts forward an opposition of the Bible and the stories of pagans. What must Mahometans think of us and our Gospel? 'Will they not be apt to say that surely we ourselves believe it no better than a Fable?' That he was not alone was manifest when *Messiah* proved to be 'indifferently relish'd' in London in Lent 1743. It did no better at its revival in 1745. It was not until 1750 that *Messiah* attracted real applause. That year, as at the first performance in Dublin, Handel associated the oratorio with a charity: he gave it as a benefit for the Foundling Hospital.

People liked buying tickets for concerts that benefited the orphans. They liked seeing the little girls and boys in their neat uniforms sitting in their rows at the performances. It all did them good. They felt better. They liked to think that they were just the sort of people Handel meant them to be. They invented an anecdote of Lord Kinnoull's congratulating Handel on 'the noble entertainment' he had given the town and of the composer's replying that 'I should be sorry if I only entertained them, I wish to make them better'. Handel was too good a Lutheran to put his trust in the betterment of women and men. He hoped, rather, that they should better appreciate the wonder of what God was doing.

In *Messiah* he had achieved that ambition of making a music which should touch the hearts, imaginations and minds of his hearers, which had eluded him in *Israel in Egypt*. Whatever the da capo echoes, whatever the ecclesiastical tone of a great many sections of *Messiah*, Handel has managed to break the bounds of both proscenium and roodscreen, and make a direct appeal to his listener. The startling exhortation at the very beginning is addressed with real immediacy to the lady in the box and the boy in the gallery: 'Comfort ye'. His working of Jennens' text is from the beginning directed towards bringing the music home personally to each member of his audience, and at the same time, towards enabling each to appreciate herself or himself as sharing an experience as audience, as Christians, as human race. 'Comfort' is announced to 'people'. Those who know their own 'iniquity' share an experience with all who are 'pardon'd'. The return of the phrase in the orchestra, after the tenor's English words, allows the dullest-eared listener to repeat it, not aloud, not consciously at all perhaps, but making it the listener's own. Then each one is engaged by the sprightliness of 'exalted'. Handel's tune is an invitation to the dance. Here, if anywhere, is the music to corroborate the story of Handel's telling Gluck that 'what the English like is something they can beat time to, something that hits them straight on the drum of the ear'. Something, we might have added before the uncivilizing shower unit spoilt all such things, to sing in the bath. Something, we may still add, at the music which so nicely imitates the 'crooked' and 'plain' of the Messiah's road, to grin to each other about. Quite naturally, it must seem, though it is a work of sophistication, Handel brings us in the first three numbers of *Messiah* to that sharing of our neighbour's condition which is musically figured in a chorus of all voices, 'and all flesh shall see it together'.

We are readied by this beginning to realize our part in the Chorus's announcement that 'Unto us' a child is born, that he hath borne 'our griefs', and with his stripes 'we are healed', so that we enjoy the liberation which is being divinely effected. 'Let us break their bonds asunder, and cast away their yokes from us.' That liberation is given the necessary musical emphasis to make it possible for us to believe in the conversion that Butler looked for: 'we shall be chang'd'. These choral affirmations constitute the proper expression of the listeners' response to the good news. Walpole had a sense of what Handel was doing, and, typically, tried to mock it away: 'The Oratorios thrive abundantly', he wrote to his almost equally tiresome crony Horace Mann in March 1743, 'for my part they give me an idea of heaven, where everybody is to sing whether they have voices or not'.

There is a story that in composing *Messiah* Handel 'did think' that he 'did see God' in his heaven. If this is an authentic anecdote then it may seem that we have to decide whether Handel was letting slip a hint of some mystical experience occasioned by the awed sense of what he was composing, or whether he was slipping back into the habit of a lifetime as a theatrical man, and 'seeing' God as a character on the stage of his mind, just as he had 'seen' Apollo or Cleopatra. But these are not necessarily alternatives. A spiritual experience of even the most mystical sort occurs in a way that is appropriate to the spirit of the experiencer. For Handel, any 'seeing' of God would be within the usual uses of his mind, within, that is, the dramatic, theatrical conditions which always obtained when he was most intensely engaged. If, say, St Catherine spoke in French to Joan of Arc, if it were in a Yarmouth herring that Julian of Norwich touched the blood of Christ, Handel would, if he were to see God, see God in the theatrical terms of his own experiencing.

In those theatrical terms, God is the chief actor in the drama of events, the protagonist of the salvation history of the race and of the individual self. When Mrs Cibber was given recitatives and arias to sing that declare the liberating history for the race, Mrs Maclaine, the soprano of the first performance, made the distinct announcement of the personal significance of that history in the most wondrous and easily appreciated music of the oratorio. Handel had at last come to his sister's favourite passage: 'I know that my Redeemer liveth'. That personal significance of knowing and being liberated depends on the Redeemer's action within the race. But if the meaning of *Messiah* is that God is active in our history, and that we ourselves are brought actively into a personal engagement with God, then the form of *Messiah* is insufficiently representative of such dramatic action.

John Brown (1715–66) noted in his dissertation on the *Rise, Union and Power . . . of Poetry and Music* in 1763, that *Messiah*, 'though that grand Musical Entertainment is termed "an Oratorio", yet it might more properly be classified as a collection of *Hymns* or *Anthems*'. He was indicating a relation between what Handel was doing in *Messiah* and *Israel in Egypt*, the music for the funeral of Queen Caroline, and for King George's coronation. If Humphreys had prevented the exposition of the divine dynamic of salvation, he had left the composer scope for the exploration of human behaviour. Jennens had prevented Handel from representing both the progressive activity of the divine in the world and the developing interaction of human beings with their Lord. Whatever Jennens meant by his remark in 1754 that *Messiah* was 'a fine entertainment' but 'not near as good as he might & ought to have done', he did not mean that he himself should have provided a more *Saul*-like libretto. Handel kept Jennens ignorant of his plans for his next oratorio. 'Whether I shall do something in the Oratorio way', he wrote to him in September 1742, 'I can not determine as yet.' Before the middle of October he had finished his revision of *Samson*.

Samson (1743)

After *Messiah*, even before he went to Ireland, Handel had begun work on *Samson*. He was looking for a way of dramatizing the contemplative structures of *Messiah*. He knew that his talents were theatrical and that he would have to find a theatrical form which would enable him still to concentrate an audience's attention at a point where the scriptural guidance was recognizably appropriate to their experience. He had to demonstrate the presence of a Zoroastro for their Orlando-like anxiety. He settled, a little surprisingly perhaps, on Milton's *Samson Agonistes*, which was so little regarded as a drama by Handel's contemporaries that Bishop Atterbury had once suggested to Pope that he adapt it for the stage. Handel recognized that Milton had been, in Dalila, Manoa and, most especially, Harapha, as inventive as Racine in *Athalie*. *Samson Agonistes* would allow him to remake his dramatic path to scriptural oratorio.

Milton himself had understood the need for careful thought before attempting to make the scriptural story into a play. He had found the structural paradigms of his drama in the *Oedipus at Colonus* of Sophocles and the *Prometheus Bound* of Aeschylus: 'Tragedy as it was antiently compos'd', he instructed his readers,

> hath been ever held the gravest, moralist, and most profitable of all other poems: therefore said by Aristotle to be of power by raising pity and fear, or terror, to purge the mind of those and such like passions, that is to temper and reduce them in just measure with a kind of delight, stirr'd up by reading or seeing those passions well imitated.

The Christian pedigree of what he was doing is illustrated by Gregory Nazianzen's thinking it 'not unbecoming the sanctity of his person to write a Tragedy which he entitled *Christ Suffering*'.

There had been a long tradition of seeing Samson as a figure of Christ, stretching from Ambrose to Augustine, through mediaeval commentators, Rupert of St Heribert being perhaps the most elaborate, to Milton's own contemporaries.[5] Thomas Hayne in his *General View of the Holy Scriptures* (1640) had printed lengthy lists of features paralleled in the stories of Samson and of Christ. Someone, not his librettist Newburgh Hamilton (1704–59), may have pointed out to Handel the popular allegory, preserved by Hayne among many others, of Samson's lifting the gates of Dan as a figure of that harrowing of Hell gates celebrated at the start of *La Resurrezione*.

Samson, if heard as a member of that Christological tradition of 'allegory', 'shadow' and 'type', would constitute a rejoinder to deist canons of exegesis, reinvoking that Butlerian world in which Samson had his place, as he had in Hebrews 11, between Barak and Jephthah. But Handel was also rescuing Samson's significance from the rationalist exegesis of the orthodox. From, for example, the kind of *Commentary upon the Books of Joshua, Judges and Ruth* published by Bishop Simon Patrick in 1702, in which Samson is reduced to a master of hounds organizing a fox hunt 'in which his Servants and Neighbours and Friends no doubt assisted him'. Handel is reaffirming story against both deist and orthodox reductionism.

He was ready to take any assistance that Sophocles, Milton or anyone else could offer him in the creation of the 'gravest' work of art which should be 'profitable' because it seized the imaginations and prompted self-scrutiny in those who attended its performance. But if Milton was an obvious choice as a guide to English biblical oratorio construction, Newburgh Hamilton was not at all the first man that would have come to mind if talk had turned to a survey of Miltonic librettists. Handel's previous oratorio, *Messiah*, and his previous attempts at Miltonic verse, *L'Allegro* and *Il Penseroso*, had been made in the company of Jennens. But Handel now seemed to be deliberately avoiding him. And Jennens exploded when he heard that *Samson*, taken from the work of his own favourite poet, was to be performed on 18 February 1743, before anyone in London had heard *Messiah*. He could not understand Handel's 'neglect of *Messiah*' and his preferring 'the Nonsense foisted by one Hamilton into Milton's *Samson Agonistes*'. What 'one Hamilton' had put together was not, however, 'Nonsense'.

Hamilton's own sense of what he was doing is declared in his preface to the first printing of the libretto. He indicates a line running from tragedy 'after the manner of the Antients', through Milton's writing a play that was not for the stage, to Handel's invention of oratorio, which he calls 'a musical Drama' in which 'the Solemnity of Church-Musick is agreeably united with the most pleasing Airs of the Stage'. Handel had something more substantially dramatic than those 'pleasing Airs' when he settled to what he had been given in Hamilton's text.

Samson is himself the dramatic presence of Handel's leading idea in *Samson*. After the 'bondage' and 'burden' of a distant past in *Israel in Egypt*, and the 'bonds' and 'yokes' of a timeless suffering in *Messiah*, Samson is dragged out before us in chains, blinded, humiliated. Nothing in 'they made them serve with rigour' or even in 'He was despised' touches us so nearly as this.

Samson is brought from being 'captive, poor, and blind', through the endurance of 'a slave half-slain', to the death which 'hath paid his ransome'. Manoah had, at the end, been negotiating 'to work his liberty'. Micah encouraged 'hopes of his delivery'. But 'captive', 'slave' and 'ransome' are referred in Handel's music to a release of Samson's 'very inmost mind'. This music renews for the hearers what they already know of an inward captivity, a darkness of the spirit. And it offers a hope of release: *Samson* promises 'liberty to all opprest'.

When Butler lay dying, it was just this bringing together of scriptural testimony and Christian actuality that he could not effect for himself: 'I never felt its virtue'. Handel has found his way through the narrative to a dramatic declaration of immediate power. Hamilton had not, however, given that necessary emphasis to 'ransome' which would have enabled Handel to proceed to some further exploration of the connection between being 'opprest' and coming into 'liberty'. Hamilton did not give any sign that a divine liberation might be given to the sufferer through suffering. He remained, indeed, content to convert *Samson Agonistes* into a merely deistical rhyme:

> Just are the ways of God
> And justifiable to men

had been turned into an echo of the opening of Epistle II of Pope's *Essay on Man*:

> Just are the ways of God to man
> Let none his secret actions scan.

A more Miltonic reference to that tradition of Samson as a prefigure of the Christ might have prompted an emphasis on 'ransome'. A reference to that tradition might, Miltonically also, in presenting a relation between Hercules and the Christ, have helped him here to formulate the analogy to which Handel's enterprise was bringing him.

Butler had presented an analogy in which the obscurity of natural phenomena is to God's processes in nature what the obscurity of the scriptural revelation is to God's processes in grace. There is already within Handel's work the outline of a further analogy of story: the light of the scriptural revelation is to a freedom God offers in grace what the light of a mythic story is to a freedom God offers in nature. Butler expected the same mystification from revelation as from the physical universe: each would present a mysterious character to the human observer because each expresses the mystery of God's mind and will for creation. Handel expects the same enlightenment from the myths as from the scriptural revelation. He would have us read, appreciate and retell both forms of narrative in the well-founded hope of enjoying a larger experience of God. Each will have its revealing power. Each will be liberating.

The audience for myth

Handel decided that before he could articulate his analogy of myth and Scripture he would have to make two preliminary announcements. First, he would have to make his audience well aware of how seriously he was taking the mythic narratives and thus how seriously he expected them to take his account of what was going on in the myths. He was not going to have them dismiss myth as 'mere myth'. Second, he would have to see to it that those who were already acquainted with the traditional material did not assume that there would be nothing new for them in his retelling. He was not going to have them dismiss an oratorio as 'mere repetition'. The first of these preliminaries is rehearsed in *Semele*, and the second in *Joseph and his Brethren*.

Semele (1744)

After the first-night disaster of *The Way of the World* at Lincoln's Inn Fields in 1700, William Congreve wrote nothing for the theatre except, as Leigh Hunt put it, 'a prologue or so, and one or two miserable bits of operas'. Originally, Congreve seems to have intended his *Semele* libretto to be part of an English challenge to the Italian opera. But that battle was lost before he and Eccles could produce their *Semele*. The text waited, unsung, for Handel to take it up in 1743.

On 4 May 1743, Walpole, always eager to help a piece of gossip on its way, was reporting that 'Handel has had a palsy and can't compose'. He had indeed had another stroke. Mainwaring talks of 'some return of his paralytic disorder'. But he began *Semele* on 3 June and had completed it by 4 July. 'The Story of Semele' was presented at Covent Garden on 10 February 1744, 'after the Manner of an *Oratorio*'. Mainwaring thought it 'an English opera, but call'd an Oratorio'.

Taking his starting point in Ovid's *Metamorphoses*, Congreve tells the story of Jupiter's affair with Semele, daughter of King Cadmus of Thebes, with some elegance and a good sense of dramatic pace. Jupiter carries off the girl from a marriage about to be solemnized with Prince Athamas, and sets her up in a pleasant love nest. It is at this idyllic moment that Handel inserted Pope's 'Where'er you walk'. But then, at the cunning prompting of the enraged wife, Juno, the foolish Semele asks if she may see the amorous god 'as he really is'. Girl and love nest go up in flames at the epiphany. The reality of 'endless blaze' destroys her.

There has been some notorious hunting after *Semele*'s meaning. Alfred Heuss in 1914 suggested that Handel's music told a story of the peculiar hubris of the female who seeks to possess her male too entirely.[6] But Congreve and Handel each appreciated, as *Love for Love* and *Samson* exemplify, that if a text is to carry a meaning effectively it must carry it at various levels. And though it could be argued that an inappropriate desire for possession of the male is exhibited in Juno and in Semele's sister Ino, as well as Semele herself, the story equally suggests an inappropriateness in the feelings of Jupiter and Athamas. The one is creating a dangerous imbalance in their relation which Semele cannot be expected to sustain, the other is conspiring with her father to confine Semele within a marriage she does not want. The consistent tone of the work is not a dread of the demanding female but the disappointment and frustration at the general human ability to fall in love with the wrong person.

Congreve's text and, by derivation, Handel's music drama, should also be construed as a consideration of the hubris of a human being who would possess a divinity. The comparison here would not be with the Elsa and Lohengrin story that Heuss adduced, but with those fetishists of the African tribes which were then figuring in coffee-house arguments about religion, or with the refusal of the Lord in the burning bush to give his name to Moses, or with the distressing fate of Uzzah in 2 Samuel 6. At the final entry of Jupiter in all his glory, Semele cannot deal with the god. She dies admitting her inadequacy: 'I can no more'. And we are not offered any advice on the maintenance of safe relation with the divine. Just when we expect a clarifying ending which will declare how we are to comprehend the events which have been presented in the drama, the drama comes to a sudden, unhelpful stop.

Once the chorus has seen Semele being burnt up in the presence of Jupiter, they express what they have been taught by their nannies, but in the astronomical language they think suitable to divinities:

> Nature to each allots his proper sphere
> But that forsaken we like meteors err.

On such an assumption, it seems wrong to worry about the fate of the girl who loved above her station. It begins to seem quite right that Juno should be 'in her chariot ascending'. The class conventions of the cosmos have so quickly reasserted themselves that the chorus can, rather indelicately, employ an image of Semele's recent fate in their acknowledgement that they have misjudged the situation:

> all our boasted fire is lost in smoke.

We are, as we listen, assumed to have entirely forgotten what has happened. Everything is hidden behind this smokescreen. Athamas is married off to Ino. A newer and nicer divinity appears in the sky. Apollo promises the birth of a baby god who shall 'sighing and sorrow for ever prevent'. For the first time in the music drama, the trumpets sound. The chorus now declares *Semele* to be a delightful entertainment and refuses to dwell on the unfortunate past, or on the dangers in the future from baby Dionysus. We are, unthinkingly, invited to join the party. The chorus raises a pleasing song for us all to enjoy:

> Happy, happy, shall we be,
> Free from care, from sorrow free,
> Guiltless pleasures we'll enjoy
> Virtuous love will never cloy;
> All that's good and just we'll prove
> And Bacchus crown the joys of love.

We should surely be uncomfortable at so cheery an end being put to so terrible a story. It is at our discomfort that Handel is aiming. He is hoping to make us aware, despite ourselves, of the way in which we so often respond to the recital of what happens in a myth. It is, we say, just a story; and stories, unlike life, should have happy endings. That is why we like to tell them. Handel is making us ask ourselves if we should so easily dismiss the myth that he has been putting before us in *Semele*.

Congreve's ending conveys that sophisticated and gifted man's belief that we are incapable of tragedy, that our lives are no more than farce. Handel's meaning, however it shifts from one music drama to another, is never that human love and life are pointless. Here he has turned

Congreve's ending into a mirror in which, seeing ourselves in the feckless, unfeeling chorus, we may be jolted into some eagerness for a more humane existence.

Joseph and his Brethren (1744)

Three weeks after the first performance of *Semele* in February 1744, Handel was presenting *Joseph and his Brethren*. These two works have the appearance of forming a pair, not in musical form or dramatic style, but in their contribution to the composer's declaration of his analogy of myth and scriptural revelation. They have that appearance, too, in their deliberate alienation of the audience at a critical moment of the action.

It may well be that the story of Joseph had been brought to Handel's notice by a recent contribution to the continuing debate about Old Testament prophecy. Thomas Morgan, just before his death in 1743, had completed a *History of Joseph* in which he had engaged with the Nonconformist Samuel Chandler (1693–1766), who had set out to offer a *Defence of the Prime Ministry and Character of Joseph*, which was also published in the year that Handel began work on *Joseph and his Brethren*. He had taken up yet another scriptural topic which was being tossed about in contemporary conversation.

Handel's choice of the Reverend James Miller's libretto was certainly not made on account of any likeness to the elegancies of Congreve's *Semele* text. Miller provided a dullish set of verses, and he was not good at telling a straightforward story. In Act I, after Joseph has interpreted the Pharaoh's dream and warned him of thin times coming, he is made overseer of the economy, given a new name, and married to the Pharaoh's daughter Asenath. We have then to assume, before the start of Act II, that Joseph's brethren have come from Canaan, collected their corn and returned home, leaving Simeon as a hostage until they shall bring Benjamin to greet Joseph. These things assumed, the Act actually begins with Asenath self-questioningly lamenting that she cannot make Joseph happy. It continues with the imprisoned Simeon not understanding how it is that, after a year, the brethren have not returned to release him. Neither wife nor brother can comprehend Joseph's interest in the family. Nor do they understand, when Benjamin is at last produced at court, why Joseph should burst into tears. At the start of Act III Asenath is concluding that Joseph falsely suspects her of loving someone else. She does not know how to deal with his mistake. The Act continues with the brethren's ignorant amazement at the cup discovered in Benjamin's baggage. Puzzlement is everywhere. And Miller, it seems, meant us to identify with these characters in their unknowing. But we cannot.

It is not because the oratorio tells a well-known story that we feel we know what is happening and what is going to happen. If there is a willing suspension of disbelief there can also be a suspension of knowledge. The excitement of the trial scene in *The Merchant of Venice* may be somewhat different for us the first time we see the play from all subsequent times, but every time we both know and do not know what is going to happen to Antonio. Shakespeare demands that we experience the story anew as the play is being performed. Handel proved himself quite capable of making this demand effectively in *Giulio Cesare*, in *Saul*, and in the recent *Samson*. But in listening to *Joseph and his Brethren* we do not sense that demand. Handel allows us to return from the oratorio to consult our memories of Genesis. He allows us, that is, to pride ourselves on recognizing the action and the significance of the action. When we hear expressions of ignorance from Asenath or Benjamin we sit back comfortably, assured that such ignorance will be cleared up soon and turned to happiness. But those who pride themselves on knowing are to get a shock.

However well we know the story, we are not prepared for the reverberation of 'Impostor!' when Joseph denounces Simeon as a spy. We are suddenly conscious of something happening in their relationship which we could not have forecast from Genesis. The emotional impact of the music startles us from any complacent assumption that we comprehend what all these characters are like. We are suddenly as much in the dark as any of them. We have identified with Joseph. We have, like him, believed that we understood all that there was to be understood. But now Joseph does not understand. He knows nothing of what Simeon has had to bear since the brethren first told the lie about Joseph's death.

The music commandeers our attention for Simeon. We are forced, uninformedly, tentatively, clumsily, to put things together in a wholly unexpected way. Handel is ensuring that we surrender our previous reading of the story. We are to feel with Simeon the burden of the imposture. We are to shudder with him in his shame at all the lies and deceits and pretences of life. We are to squirm in confused recognition of a wretchedness that forces itself into expression at 'ah, my foul offence'.

No new knowledge will convert Simeon's misery into an easily greeted joy. His shudder will not be lessened by a discovery that Joseph knows all about his past. His shame can only be brought to its end by his being forgiven. This is the dramatic importance of 'Thou hadst, my lord, a father once' in Act III at which Joseph's knowledge meets Simeon's feeling. Simeon's offer to stay in prison if Benjamin can return to their father becomes the occasion of liberation. Joseph forgives him. Simeon is freed from shame, from ignorance, and from prison bars. And, in forgiving his brother, Joseph is himself freed from imprisoning bitterness.

After such forgiveness the brethren share a full knowledge of what has been happening. Everything that any one of them knew or thought he knew seems different now. Whatever the audience thought they knew before Handel retold the story, they know differently now. Whatever they know of the facts of a history, the wonders of a mythic narrative, or the chapter and verse of a scriptural narrative, they have learnt that they still have something to learn. They must listen to the story-teller. To Handel.

Though the singer of Joseph was 'a block with a very fine voice', and the Simeon had 'no voice at all', the oratorio took with the public. Covent Garden was satisfyingly full at each performance. Handel decided that his audience was now ready to hear that analogy of Myth and Scripture which he had been so long preparing.

Theologies and liberation: *Hercules* (1745)

It is remarkable that Handel does not seize the obvious chance of emphasizing the likeness of the mythic Hercules to the scriptural Samson. Stillingfleet had thought it 'very probable' that 'the memory' of Samson 'was preserved under Hercules Tyrius'.[7] But there is nothing in *Hercules* about killing lions, nothing, in this retelling of the last day of the hero's life, and his finally being brought down by his wife, which would prompt a hearer's remembrance of Samson.

Nor was Handel making a quick reference to the patristic tradition of Hercules as the 'type' or 'shadow' of Christ as a hero struggling against the powers of death. In Freylinghausen's Halle songbook, the resurrection Lord had been hymned in a series of heroic verses as a 'conquering hero' who reduces 'the power of death to naught'.[8] But whatever his own appreciation of this typological language, there is no sign that Handel was expecting more than a civilized hearer's passing recognition of such a tradition in *Hercules*.

Nor did Handel have explicit recourse to that likening of Hercules to Christian champions which he had also known since his Halle childhood. There was a well-known Protestant usage of the Hercules figure. Giordano Bruno had written of Luther as 'the new Alcides'. Zwingli had been hailed as 'Hercules Helviticus'. The Tudor courtier Sir Anthony Coke had greeted Henry VIII as the Hercules who slew 'the Romayne monster Hydra'. These things were subject to changes of fashion. Handel may well have known that Bruno altered his mind about Luther and decided that the real Hydra lay concealed within 'justification by faith alone'. And he may have known that the Papist Giraldi had celebrated the Herculean character of that Catholic champion, the Holy Roman Emperor Charles V.[9] Whatever resonances of the Christian tradition of Hercules might be heard in this oratorio by individual members of his audience, Handel did not want to obscure the mythic character of his story-telling. Hamilton was quite mistaken when he assured the reader of his *Samson* preface that oratorio was a form of art 'whose Subject must be Scriptural'. Handel's analogy of Myth and Scripture in his oratorio writing depended for its operation on the hearer's appreciating the peculiar wonder of a myth. The story of Hercules was now to declare its relevance to the life of the most ordinary hearer.

Newburgh Hamilton had been enthusiastic for oratorio 'after the manner of the Antients', but if Handel this time expected a faithful, if updated to 1744, version of Sophocles' *Trachiniae*, he was mistaken in his new librettist.

Broughton and Ovid's *Metamorphoses*

Thomas Broughton (1704–74) was a man whose serious theological interests mark him out from Handel's previous colleagues. Humphreys had been a Cannons poetaster who published in 1735 some very dull *Annotations on the Old and New Testament*; his only other literary effort had been in translating a set of French *Peruvian Tales* and providing librettos for operas about *Poro, Re dell' indie* and *Sosarme, Re di Media*. Jennens also had ambitions to be a poet, as his impertinent addition of *Il Moderato*, for Handel to set with Milton's *L'Allegro* and *Il Penseroso*, witnesses. He thought himself a competent editor of *King Lear*. But his Non-Juror sympathies seem to have kept him from contemporary theological discussion. Whereas Miller, though always anxious to obtain some ecclesiastical preferment, could not keep himself long enough away from the theatre to write anything of theological respectability. A volume of Miller's sermons was put together by his widow. It does not repay a morning's reading in the British Museum, proving even less theologically interesting than his translation of Voltaire's play *Mahomet the Impostor*.

Broughton had made his own contribution to the second deist debates with *Christianity distinct from the Religion of Nature*, published in 1732 in three pamphlet parts as 'answer to a late book entitled *Christianity as old as the Creation*'. He had made some lively fun of Tindal's expertise in 'the noble science of Tautology', and he had had some sharp things to say about 'the mask of pretended Friendship' being in Tindal's prose 'too thin a disguise to cover and conceal the Real Foe'.[10] Broughton's main contention is that Christianity is not, as Tindal maintained, the republication of Natural Religion because Natural Religion had proved too rare a wonder for defective human understanding. The 'positive Institutions of Religion' had been designed by God to supply an aid to understanding and practice just where human 'Wants and Exigencies' require it. Broughton has a rather King-like image of 'a Prince framing Laws for his own Kingdom' who adapts another country's code to the peculiar circumstances of his own subjects. Christianity is such an adaptation of Natural Religion, 'without contradicting it'.[11] Like King and like Browne, Broughton favours optical imagery. He enjoys his own little analogy of the light of nature being to our understanding as the light of the sun is to the blind man's eye. But he is more sensitive than either King or Browne to a scriptural author's uses of metaphor. And he had, as he tackled Tindal's dismissive remarks about the corrupt tradition of the Gospel, begun to employ a 'probability' which anticipated both Butler's terminology and his meaning.

Once Butler had published his *Analogy*, orthodox controversialist efforts, Broughton's among them, remained generally unread. Broughton got himself back into public notice with his *Bibliotheca historico-sacra* in two massive volumes (1737 and 1739) which, hoping perhaps for a larger readership, he had reissued in 1742 with the translated title *An Historical Dictionary*, and the explanatory subtitle announcing that his work dealt with 'the principal matters relating to religion antient and modern'. The work is made up of an alphabetically arranged set of entries, most of them quite short, for the gods, beliefs, priesthoods, religious societies, rituals and superstitions of a great range of religions.

Broughton had read widely in the new literature of comparative religion as well as in those classical authors from whom he took his notices of Greek and Roman religion. He had read not only commentators and systematizers, Stillingfleet, Vossius and della Valle, but the original accounts of merchants and missionaries.

In tackling the terrible questions of the colonial system, Butler had argued from principles of 'charity' and 'neighbourhood', and from a general awareness of all the various Americans living in 'their country'. Broughton was more particularly informed about the original inhabitants of the places where Europeans had made their settlements. He knew about 'the Genii of Caribee Islands', 'the idolatrous Floridans', 'the savages of Virginia', and Michapous, 'whom the savages in some parts of North America call god'.[12] He had read La Potterie's *History of North America*. He knew about the Negambo priests from Cavazzi's *Istoriale descrizione da Congo*, about the Juhle spirits from Keisler's *Antiquités Celtiques* and Schaeffer's *History of Lapland*. He knew exactly what was going on when Toland produced his version of de la Créquinière's thesis of the likeness of beliefs and practices among the East Indians to those described in the Pentateuch.

He was not quite as widely read in contemporary British literature. Preparing his answer to Tindal, he had had to read Locke's *Essay Concerning Humane Understanding* rather carefully; he knew his way around Clarke's arguments; he had skimmed through Newton *On the Prophecies*. He had a gentleman's enthusiasm for *Paradise Lost*, Addison's *Essays*, and Pope's translation of Homer. And he had just published a critical edition of Dryden's poems.

Broughton's temper is, indeed, always that of a civilized Western European. He is entirely at home in the mythologies of Greece, referring to Zeus simply, as he had been taught at Eton and Cambridge, as 'king of the gods', and to Aphrodite as 'the goddess of love'. He is not at home in the religions of other cultures, referring distancingly to Devandiren as 'King of the gods according to the superstitious belief of the East Indian Pagans', and to Mango-Capac as 'a false god of the idolatrous Peruvians'. Still, he is rather more graciously tolerant of the strangenesses in the Roman Church than a great many of his Anglican contemporaries. He has entries in the *Dictionary* for a number of small communities of Italian nuns, he is precise in his account of the 'Forty Hours' devotion, he is studiously courteous in prefixing 'saint' to almost all recently canonized persons, making a silent exception only for Ignatius Loyola. He clearly knows a lot about the history of St Francis Xavier and the Jesuit missions in India and China; detailing the disputes about the Christianization of native cults and customs, he is, expectedly, disposed to support the Roman authorities. It is unfortunate that his admiring account of St Philip Neri and the Oratory has merely a passing reference to those 'hymns to the glory of God' from which oratorio developed.[13]

Broughton must have seemed to Handel to be just that large-minded, theologically informed, civilizedly literate librettist whom he had been seeking. In his debate with Tindal, Broughton had developed an account of religious 'memorials' of divine action which covered Greek, Hebrew and Christian 'institutions'. He referred to Greek 'memorials' of 'those Gods on earth' who had done them great good. Similarly the Sabbath was 'a memorial of the Creation of the World';

and the Eucharist 'a perfect memorial of the Death and Sufferings' of Christ. He was able to write easily of the congruent effects of these 'memorials'. 'If then the Hero is warmed by the example of Caesar, the Patriot by that of Brutus, can the Christian faint in the race of Virtue when so bright an Exemplar of it is set before him?'[14] There is in all this not only a feeling for the analogy of myth and Scripture which Handel was advancing, but further, a feeling that this analogy was best proposed, as Handel was proposing it in these oratorios, through exemplars.

In the *Dictionary* Broughton had collected serviceable notices of the subjects that had interested Handel in his search for exemplars. Apollo's hiring himself as a shepherd to Admetus, for example, and the god's pursuit of Daphne. There was a quite lengthy entry for 'the credulous nymph' Semele and the 'inconstancy of Jupiter' who was 'forever engaged in some amour or other'. It cannot have lessened Handel's expectations if, on looking up Broughton's notice of the life of Hercules, he discovered the simple statement that 'it was his heroic courage and constancy of mind that raised him to the dignity of a god'.[15] Though this entry ought to have warned him that the librettist, however he advertised the taking of his text from the *Trachiniae*, was not going to be an absolute follower of Sophocles' treatment of the hero and his death.

The *Trachiniae* tells the story of the last day in the lives of Heracles and his wife Deianeira. The action takes place in the forecourt of their home at Trachis. When the play begins, Deianeira has just decided to send their son Hyllus to find out what has happened to his father, since he has been away without any word to them for a year. Before Hyllus can set off, news arrives that Heracles is now on his way home. He has sent his herald before him as an escort for the captive princess Iole. Heracles had wanted to make her his concubine a year ago, but her father had objected. In his anger, Heracles ambushed her brother and tossed him off a cliff to his death. The gods, in their turn, had punished him with a year's hard labour. Heracles, feeling that somehow this was all the old king's fault, had sacked his city, murdered the father and grabbed the girl. He would be home, the herald says, as soon as he had made his thank-offering for victory at the altar of Zeus.

Deianeira looks to the future. She sees the old wife being neglected and the new concubine taking her place in the hero's life. Sophocles' Deianeira is a most delicate lady. She does not get angry with the princess; she simply sends the herald back with a present for Heracles. It is a magic shirt. Long ago a dying centaur had promised that, if her husband wore this, it would enkindle a flame of passion for her. The shirt has indeed a terrible inflaming power. But the centaur had lied. He hated them both. Hyllus comes back to tell the citizens that when Heracles put on the shirt it began to burn its way into his flesh. In his agony the hero threw the herald over a cliff to his death. The boy rounds on his mother as a murderess. Deianeira sees how she has been tricked into destroying the man she loves. She goes into the house and stabs herself, just before Heracles is borne on to the stage, screaming in pain and anger against his wife. The hero discovers the truth. The law of Zeus is that we get what we bring on ourselves, and that we bring it on others. His son places him on his funeral pyre. The rest is silence.

Broughton was fond of illustrating his *Dictionary* entries with quotations from Ovid in the translations of Dryden and Addison, and in constructing his *Hercules* text for Handel he proved to be rather more impressed by Ovid than by Sophocles as a plot-maker. Broughton seized on Ovid's vulgar suggestion, in the ninth book of the *Metamorphoses*, that Deianeira was all the time motivated by an unjust suspicion that Iole was the mistress of Heracles. Rewriting the story from this alien angle, Broughton altered its balance.

Broughton's libretto keeps with the general line of Sophocles' play only for the first Act. Act II is mainly his own invention. There Iole, alone in a strange land, is interrogated by the accusing Dejanira. The innocent princess cannot prevent the onset of the wife's jealousy. After the hatred of Hercules's wife, Iole has next to deal with the loving attentions of his son. Hyllus says that he wants to marry her: he talks of nothing but the power of love to bring gods down from Olympus to catch such a bride. Here the chorus, as unthinking as most of Handel's choruses, sings of the 'wanton god of amorous fires', as if Semele had never got burnt.

Dejanira, having taxed Hercules as well as Iole and being unconvinced by his denials, sends the shirt as a love token to revive his affections. Broughton's management of this incident suggests that she is somehow aware of the terrible power within the shirt: that what is to happen has somehow been willed by Dejanira. By the start of Act III, Hercules has been horribly scorched by the centaur's blood whose poisonous power has been roused by the heat of the altar fires. The herald describes how the hero has fallen 'inglorious', struck down 'by a woman's hand'. The chorus keens the death of 'the world's avenger', and the dying Hercules is carried into the forecourt.

The Ovidian motivation which Broughton has taken for his plotting of the oratorio is now complemented by the librettist's own sense that a jealousy such as drove Dejanira to send the shirt must be punished. This is his characteristic reaction. The essay on the 'Penalties' for sin placed as an 'Appendix' to his first pamphlet against Tindal was almost as long as his rebuttal of the deist's whole argument about natural and revealed religion. Whilst writing *Hercules*, he was already engaged in those considerations of physical and psychological torments in eternity which would constitute a large part of his 1768 treatise on the *Prospect of Futurity*. Dejanira is driven mad by the arrival of demons from the hereafter.

As the jealous wife descends into madness, the hero is received into heaven. The gods issue their decree for the future government of his kingdom: they command Hyllus and Iole to marry and reign. Broughton's story concludes with everyone joining in a grand hymn to the great liberator who is now enthroned in the skies.

In altering the thrust of Sophocles' action, Broughton has altered the character of the god who orders the universe in which the action is going forward. The Zeus who commanded an inexorably just order within which Heracles' rough stuff brought disaster on all who were caught up in his career, guilty and innocent alike, has become some quite other sort of god. He has become a god who reckons the intentions of women and men into his accounts, who reckons, indeed, their unconscious desires. A god who defends the innocent and sees to it that they end up happier than the guilty. A god who, at last, welcomes those he loves into his heavenly kingdom. Broughton is preparing the way for the god to be God, or, at any rate, God as eighteenth-century Anglican orthodoxy pronounced God to be.

Broughton does not share the rather disturbing notion of Browne that human beings are to be examined chiefly for what they can tell us about God. He has, in the course of *Hercules*, certainly proved that he is interested in the ways our minds work. But his gradual assimilation of the god to God is not quite the analogy that Handel intends by his suggestion that there is a likeness between the myth's relation to our experience and the scriptural story's relation to our experience. His oratorio has, therefore, not quite the tone of Broughton's text.

Handel and the celebration of liberty

Broughton aimed at producing a tidy piece of playwriting which should have the further advantage of delivering a respectable moral. His main instrument in this design was the development of the character of Iole.

Handel made Iole his own. He first of all takes this innocent captive as an example of what a complacent, swaggering bully-boy will do to others if he is given his way in the world. She is the political prisoner. The individual unhappiness of the captive princess is turned by Handel into a signal of the distress of all who have been thrust out of their homes and shut into a gaol or a forced labour camp:

> Captivity, like the destroyer death,
> Throws all distinctions down, and slaves are equal.

Iole is, next, a figure for Handel of those who in their imprisonment recognize that they must wait upon a divine release. He puts a deliberate musical emphasis on the single hope allowed to Iole:

> But, if the gods relent, and give us back
> To our lost liberty. . . .

To ensure that we are indeed feeling with Iole, Handel flashes back to the moment of brutality from which all this unhappiness depends:

> My father! ah, methinks I see
> The sword inflict the deadly wound.

He makes her past part of our present. Everything in the music combines to emphasize the present tense of Broughton's text:

> He bleeds, he falls in agony,
> Dying he bites the crimson ground.

The words are no more convincing than the rhetoric of Hyllus about 'the valiant chief' and his 'amorous vows', but there is a power in the music to persuade us that Iole's emotion is true. We are compelled to sympathize. We feel with Iole what it is to be powerless before such violence. This is a real response to a real terror and it cannot be sustained for long. The music changes as Handel releases us from the intensity of that emotion into which he has thrust us. The girl now prays that her father's spirit may enjoy 'peaceful rest'.

Handel develops his view of Iole through a series of Wagnerian dialogues in Act II: Iole and Dejanira, Iole and Hyllus, Iole and Dejanira again. And he has just Wagner's motive in this dialogue construction. Handel is allowing the audience to overhear him talking to himself, turning over the complexities of the situation as it occurs in his imagination. Each dialogue is dominated by a da capo aria which requires the audience to attend not to the action itself, which is very easily comprehended, but to the hidden springs of the action that are revealed as the characters come to appreciate themselves and those with whom they are compelled to act. And once we have seen what is proceeding in his mind through the relations of Iole with Dejanira and

Hyllus, Handel, again very like Wagner in this, propels the action by transferring a significant stage 'prop' from one character to another: Dejanira sends the shirt to Hercules.

The Act III 'Simfony' sets a great *largo* tune on its way and then sends a *furioso* theme crashing into it. The world is about to be cracked open. The Act begins with the return of the herald from the thanksgiving ceremony with the news of Hercules' terrible agony. Handel provides the chorus with a sequence of irreconcilable phrases which perfectly express their sense of the disintegration of their world. They look out on a frightening future, when Hercules will no longer be there to defend them. They see tyrants recovering confidence, they see people like themselves made into slaves, and, with this loss of liberty, they see the whole natural order falling back into chaos. Out of the darkness will slouch prehistoric beasts, 'horrid forms of monstrous birth', to plunder and subdue the earth. This is what their hero-worship has brought them to feel.

Then we see the hero. Cursing the woman who is murdering him, Hercules thinks himself in the worst hell, wracked 'with more than Stygian pains'. But Dejanira is more devilishly punished. Handel gives full value to the frightfulness within Broughton's verses. Monstrous forms do indeed surround her, huge enough to hide the sun. The cosmos is defiled by the filthy creatures which she has let into her conscious mind. They have crept out of their caverns in the unconscious. This is a far more terrible vision than anything foreseen by the chorus. Handel finds a music for this experience of possession, of menace everywhere, of derangement of every faculty and sense. He proves himself the master of each twist and turn the wretched woman makes in her despairing efforts to escape her madness. Any comparison with the Baroque rhetoric of Orlando or the morose bitterness of Saul is wholly irrelevant. This is madness itself.

After the howls of Hercules against a world that is treating him as he had always treated the world, after the oppressive tread of tyrants heard in the foreboding of the chorus, after the yet more primitive chaos let loose in the screams of Dejanira, Handel directs our attention to the silence of Iole at the still centre.

Out of her silence springs the loveliness of her da capo aria, 'My breast with tender pity swells'. She makes her appeal to whatever is good and loving and merciful in the order of the world. We can hear the analogy of experience in the air. There is a perfect likeness of response to mythic and scriptural story-telling: 'This', says Winton Dean, 'is the Handel of "I know that my Redeemer liveth"'.

Broughton's plot-management would seem to give Handel just the scope he requires to make that redeeming power felt. The priest returns from the sacrificial altar with the strange greeting: 'Rejoice, princess'. It is not to Iole that he speaks but to Dejanira. Her jealousy, the centaur's malice, the whole dreadful derangement of the world, have been turned to good: the gods have relented; Hercules has found happiness with his heavenly father. Broughton is a trifle wary of divinization. He allows the priest to say only that 'his part immortal' has been carried to Olympus. But even in this talk of the god, which fits so neatly with contemporary Christian talk of the soul, we may hear Broughton's excitement at a divinely willed *lieto fine* for the hero.

None of this holds much interest for Handel. He gives the priest's announcement of apotheosis no prominence in his musical design of the scene. Handel intends us to keep our ears on Iole. The priest's next words are to her: 'Nor less thy destiny . . .'. He does not mean that Iole is to become a goddess but that the god cares for her as providentially as his relenting shows him to be caring for Hercules. Handel is now preparing the marriage of Iole and Hyllus.

In a clutch of the cultures that contemporary researchers had been making known to eighteenth-century readers, it is common for women and men to have a sense of encountering the divine at the wedding as at the deathbed. It was expressed in the culture of Handel's audience through the language of 'with my body I thee worship' and 'what God has joined'. Opera had its start as a celebration connected to the Christian sacrament. And the opera performed at that marriage celebration had been an invocation of Grecian divinities. Venus and Pluto had attended when Peri's *Euridice* was performed in 1660 as part of the Medici court festivities for the proxy marriage of Henri IV and Maria de' Medici. The masque of Hymen at the wedding of Rosalind and Orlando in *As You Like It*, announcing mirth in heaven when human beings 'atone together', and the vision of goddesses that Prospero conjures for Miranda and Ferdinand in *The Tempest*, reflect similarly arranged epiphanies at Jacobean court weddings. More recently, Juno had given her heavenly approval of the marriage with which Handel had begun *Semele*. And in *Il Parnasso in Festa*, 'somewhat in the Style of Oratorio', Apollo had come at Handel's bidding with a galaxy of divinities to grace the marriage of Anne, the Princess Royal, to the Stadtholder of the Netherlands in March 1734.

Jupiter's signalling his will that Iole and Hyllus should marry is thus quite in the ordinary run of things. But it is a diversion from other tellings of this Herculean story. In the *Trachiniae*, the marriage is commanded by Heracles because he cannot bear the idea that any other than a male of his own blood should lie with Iole, 'since she has been mine'. Hyllus is horrified, but Heracles insists. He will not be thwarted by a disobedient boy. There is no suggestion that Iole has any opinion in the matter; and no suggestion of Jupiter's commanding the marriage. Nor is there any suggestion of Jupiter's interest in this matter in Ovid's version of the story. There is, indeed, no mention of the wedding at all in his Hercules episode; the marriage of Iole and Hyllus is mentioned only incidentally in a following set of stories about women in labour.

The divinely willed marriage is set up in *Hercules* as a contradiction to Hercules' understanding of human relations with the divine. Hercules was, as he donned the poisoned shirt, about to thank the god for victory over the king of Oechalia and his people. The terrible interruption of that ceremony declares, in Sophocles' telling of the story, that the gods are not willing to take credit for a murderous act of revenge by a frustrated rapist. In Broughton's text the hero has been so beautifully cleaned that the audience knows nothing of his unjustified attack on the city, nothing of rape, nothing of murder, nothing of brutal reprisal. The audience knows only of a battle and a victory. So the librettist has, quite unthinkingly, left the audience to conclude that the gods are not very keen on the conquering hero. The hero has evidently misunderstood the divine. What the god gives is not victory but liberty.

The logic of *Hercules* directs the audience towards recognizing the marriage of Iole and Hyllus as the realization of a divinely given freedom. But how is Iole to accept it freely? We all remember, because she is presented in Handel's most beautiful music in *Hercules*, that the princess has already been offered a wedding long ago, and by the most appropriate person to make the offer: the man who wants to marry her. Broughton does not recognize the difference between the first scene, when Iole had rejected the prince, and the present finale in which he is taking it for granted that she will accept him. He offers, therefore, no resolution of the human situation of that earlier scene when Hyllus' proposal was rejected:

> thinkst thou Iole can ever love
> The son of Hercules?

Love had seemed to her then 'Impossible!' Why should it now be possible for her?

Broughton ought to be providing verses here that would show the 'son of Hercules' to be innocent of any hero-worship of that bully; Hyllus should now be identified as the constant lover who can release Iole from the past. What Broughton offers is a young man on the make who sees everything coming his way: 'At once with love and empire blest'. And just when he needed to exercise a command of language for such an expression of Iole's liberation as imaginative and enlivening as that he managed for Dejanira's imprisoning madness, Broughton collapses into a set of coy conventions. Iole describes love in terms which are the very reverse of liberation. She is 'vanquish'd' and will do what the gods 'approve'.

With Hyllus' talk of 'empire' and Iole's talk of 'vanquish'd', the chorus settles down into its habitual acknowledgement of authoritarian structures. They pervert the language of 'liberty'. They sing a hymn to the god Hercules:

> To him your grateful notes of praise belong
> The theme of liberty's immortal song!

Handel can make nothing out of all this: 'The music goes to pieces'. Winton Dean suggests that the air 'and the equally insipid duet' can be cut, and that the best policy with the finale is to 'reduce it to its last forty bars'.[16] Handel himself made such cuts before the first performance. He could just about bring himself to allow the chorus to sing that horrific couplet, but he could not sit quiet at his organ bench for the four lines in praise of Hercules which followed:

> Aw'd by his name, oppression shuns the light!
> And slav'ry hides her head in depths of night.
> While happy climes to his example owe
> The blessings that from peace and freedom flow.

It must have been peculiarly disappointing to Handel that his most theologically literate librettist had proved incapable at precisely the moment when the relation of the constancy of human love to the divine gift of liberty was to be expressed.

LIBERATION AND 'A CHRISTIAN STORY', 1745-50

After the première of *Hercules* on 5 January 1745, Handel wrote to the *Daily Advertiser* acknowledging the failure of 'musical drama' to please the public, and making everyone aware of the financial distress he had incurred through 'his Endeavours to entertain' the nation. One kind reply, a couple of weeks later, expressed a hope that audiences would crowd to Handel's theatre and enable *Hercules* to 'Avenge this National Disgrace'. It was a hope that would not be fulfilled. *Hercules* was withdrawn from the Haymarket repertory. As Jennens remarked, mounting 'an English Opera call'd *Hercules*' on Saturdays, when folk would be at 'Assemblys, Drums, Routs, Hurricanes, & all the madness of Town Diversions', was sheer folly. But Handel had been insistent on the serious purpose of his enterprise. He had, he wrote, meant to join 'good Sense and significant Words to Musick', for the English language was 'so expressive of the sublimest Sentiments' and perfectly adapted to 'the full and solemn Kind of Musick'. The letter to the paper, even if it were composed by another for his signature, affirms the seriousness of Handel's purpose. He intends his music to mean something: 'good Sense', 'significant Words', 'sublimest Sentiments' indicate a programme demanding not only professional and personal dedication in the composer as he struggles with the text, but, equally, a diligence in the listener's attention to the meaning that is being communicated in the music. He was often disappointed at the lack of this diligence in his hearers.

Belshazzar (1745)

On 19 July 1744 Handel had come back from a country holiday to begin work on *Hercules*, and found Jennens' text for Act I of *Belshazzar* waiting on his desk: 'I immediately perused the Act of the Oratorio with which you favour'd me, and the little time only I had it, gives me great Pleasure'. It is to be expected that the second oratorio composed that summer would be like *Hercules* in its tone and its expression of a view of the world. Its libretto was, in fact, rather too like that which Handel had been shaping into *Hercules*, but Handel could not have realized that from the Act I text.

The text for the central scene of the action, when we are to imagine 'a banquet room adorned with the images of the Babylonian gods', 'writing on the wall', and the king 'trembling from head to foot, and his knees knocking against each other', comes quite directly from Daniel 5, and Cyrus' promise that the exiles will return to Jerusalem and be allowed to rebuild their Temple, from the opening chapters of Ezra, but for the rest Jennens had to scramble amongst Isaiah and Jeremiah, Herodotus and Xenophon, for hints of the jeering citizens on the Babylonian walls, the diversion of the river by Cyrus' Persian engineers, and a name to give Belshazzar's mother. Nitocris represents the greatest departure from the source material. Jennens made her a rather loquacious bluestocking. At the very start of *Belshazzar*, Nitocris reviews the history of the world and takes particular note of the mutability of every political structure: 'Vain fluctuating state of human empire'. With the enthusiasm of a preacher who has found a

simile which will get him through the length of a sermon, Nitocris
expounds the history of the nation state as it goes through the stages
of human life:

> First small and weak, it scarcely rears its head
> Scarce stretching out its helpless infant arms

next an adolescent striving for power and wealth, then an adult
grasping at all within its reach, and so on until 'grown old and swell'd
to bulk enormous', it falls into corruption and weakness so that 'Some
other rising pow'r advantage takes'. Then all's to do again:

> The victor state, upon her ruins rais'd
> Runs the same shadowy round of fancied greatness,
> Meets the same certain end.

However intelligent and civilized Jennens thought himself, he is here
offering Handel nothing more than Sam Humphreys offered him in
Athalia over ten years before. Handel must have felt peculiarly
uncomfortable when Jennens translated that 'certain' into 'fate' and
associated the translation with God:

> In heaven or earth who dares
> Dispute Thy pow'r? Thy will is fate.

Handel would have been convinced that something was very wrong
when it is revealed that the old empress has got this idea of God from
the prophet Daniel himself.

Everything that the prophet says about history and its course goes
quite against Handel's view of the scriptural version of our condition
in time. It was much more the sort of deistical notion expounded with
dreary sameness in Bolingbroke's *Idea of a Patriot King*. Though this
was not officially published until 1749, it was being widely circulated
in the privately printed edition sponsored by Pope in 1740. It was a
further difficulty for Handel that such a view of history was being
attributed to this particular prophet.

There had been a heated debate in England for some twenty years
about Daniel and his prophecies. Anthony Collins' *Literal Scheme of
Prophecy* had been largely occupied with the curiously precise
announcements in Daniel of what the future would be like. He hoped
to undermine all Christian appeals to Hebrew prophetic writing by
demonstrating that Daniel was put together with hindsight in the reign
of Antiochus Epiphanes. Orthodox apologists had come scurrying to
defend the prophet. They were intent on preserving the prophecies for
their Christological treatises. Samuel Chandler, for example, whose
more recent work had probably influenced the writing of *Joseph and*

his Brethren, had made his name in 1728 with a *Vindication of Daniel's Prophecies*, and his establishment namesake, Edward Chandler (?1688–1750) had spent most of his 1725 *Defence of Christianity from the Prophecies* and his 1728 *Vindication of the 'Defence of Christianity'* in asserting against Collins the usefulness of Daniel in the demonstration of a divine overseeing providence. A very similar argument from Daniel as the prophet of the Messiah occurs in Law's 1731 *Case of Reason* as a knock-down argument against Tindal.

Butler, though he recognized what others could do with Daniel, more guardedly indicated the continuing fulfilment of 'a long foregoing series of prophecy' as the race headed towards the final manifestation of divine love. He felt himself to be living now in 'the prophetic history of things still future'.[17] He had therefore no reason, as he looked to the End, to concentrate on any particular prophecy which had already been fulfilled at the first coming of the Messiah. 'Prophecy' had for him the sense of a promise of further wondrous surprise.

Handel might have responded cheerfully to a text which announced such a Butlerian view of the prophets. In his account of Daniel, however, Jennens seems to be suggesting something very like the determinist version of history and divine overseeing that Handel had rejected at the close of Broughton's *Hercules* text. The priest of Jupiter had offered Iole no more than her 'destiny', insisting that she 'submit' to the 'will' declared by his divination, and not dare complain of 'its just decrees'. For the revival of *Belshazzar* in 1751, and perhaps in the middle of the first run of performances in March 1745, Handel cut out the entire first scene. His oratorio could then go forward with quite a different tone to its presentation of the divine.

Cyrus, the Persian king, reveals at the start of the second scene that he has had a dream 'inspir'd by heav'n' in which he has learnt that his coming conquest of Babylon is designed by God to ensure that, 'without ransome', Cyrus will 'set my captives free'. Victory is towards liberation. Daniel reads in Isaiah and Jeremiah that liberty is always divinely given. And having made this sense of history and of Scripture clear to his audience, Handel has really done everything he wants to do in this oratorio. But so that the positive meaning may be better appreciated and that he may keep his promise about his 'endeavours to entertain', he has recourse now to one of the oldest devices of the dramatist.

The announcement of divine liberation is juxtaposed with its parody. Handel proposes something like the satyr play after the tragic representation of human life in an Athenian theatre, or the Second Shepherds Play in the Wakefield cycle of mediaeval mysteries, or the antimasque of Jacobean court festivities. Jennens' text gave Handel the chance of portraying the 'liberty' of Belshazzar, lurching among the revellers, whilst the wine flows 'free' in honour of Sesach, his god:

> Let order vanish, liberty alone,
> Unbounded liberty, the night shall crown.

Despite the earnestness of Jennens, the scene gets funnier as Nitocris makes an effort to rebuke her son. Handel renders her into a comic parson in a farce as she struggles to restore decency:

> Who can endure
> Th'unbridled license of this festival,
> Miscall'd by the licentious, liberty?

It is a further irony, missed by Jennens but certainly felt in Handel's setting, that, forgetting all her earlier talk of 'inevitability', Nitocris hopes that her son will reassert 'reason's empire' and save the nation. And a further irony yet that Belshazzar should return her language upon herself, accusing his mother of falling into 'the dotage of palsied age'. He refuses to waste more time 'in frivolous dispute'. Seeing the 'captive Jews', grim-faced at the feast, he accuses them, too, of envying his 'liberty', and sends for the cups of the Jerusalem Temple to hold the wine for a grand toast to Sesach. At this confrontation of liberties the music changes. The writing appears on the wall. Cyrus is heard coming ever nearer.

The theological significance of this antimasque resides in its signalling Handel's departure from his previous expressions of the Butlerian concept of a unified liberty. Handel is making a theatrically striking distinction between liberties. That he is not simply echoing the Nitocris distinction of 'liberty' from 'licentiousness' becomes clear in the last section of *Belshazzar*.

Having read thus far in the text, Handel had written to Jennens that 'Your most excellent Oratorio has furnished me with Expressions, and given me Opportunity to some very particular Ideas'. But he could not go on with any great enthusiasm as Jennens turned the whole of the last part of the libretto into a celebration of the political freedom that victory secures. Cyrus' soldiers now sing that, if only all kings were like their leader,

> Sweet liberty, beatific peace,
> Would stretch their wings from shore to shore
> And war and slav'ry be no more.

Handel was getting impatient with all this talk of such liberty being in the gift of kings and conquerors. 'You may believe', he wrote to

Jennens on receiving the final instalment of the text, 'that I think it a very fine and sublime Oratorio, only it is really too long.' He refused to make any attempt to set a passage in which Jennens associated the prophet Isaiah with satisfaction in military conquest. Handel cuts and shapes and cuts until the emphases are placed at the end of the battle on a father's tears for his dead son and the general's rejection of 'destructive war'. Handel's music in this section of the oratorio insists on the difference between the victory of Cyrus and the freeing of the Jewish captives as forcefully as he had insisted on the difference between the victory of Hercules and the freeing of Iole. But now, whilst Broughton had inhibited him in *Hercules*, he was also enabled by Jennens to make a distinction between the liberty for which a human being, Cyrus, was responsible,

> Be free, ye captives,
> And to your native land in peace return,

and the liberation of the spirit, which only God could effect. Handel was, in this, starting upon a distinction which was too nice for Jennens. But Jennens was the surer interpreter of the public's mind. Handel's audiences stayed away again. They proved themselves readier to hear of victory than of liberation.

Three patriotic noises: *Judas Maccabaeus* (1747), *Alexander Balus* (1748) and *Joshua* (1748)

In the summer of 1745 Handel was ill again. In October, Lord Shaftesbury was remarking that 'poor Handel looks something better; I hope he will entirely recover in due time, though he has been a good deal disordered in his head'. But, with Thomas Morell, a Fellow of King's College, Cambridge, Handel pulled together the dull *Occasional Oratorio*, and then agreed to work with Morell in 1746 on a *Judas Maccabaeus*. The story this time was taken from 1 Maccabees 3 – 9 and, with more circumstance, 2 Maccabees 8 – 15. Josephus gave a further account of the campaigns with some patriotic flourish in his *Antiquities of the Jews* (xii, 6–10), and Morell picked through these chapters for a few details of his libretto. He was the translator of *Hecuba* and *Prometheus Bound*, and he proved at the start of *Judas Maccabaeus* that he knew how a decent Greek might versify the sadness of captive women and the despair of defeated heroes.

The opening chorus, 'Mourn, ye afflicted', with its following half-chorus recitatives for Israelitish men and women, and the duet which then leads into the chorus 'For Sion lamentation make', was by far the most effective sequence of the text. The work is downhill all the way from this opening. The libretto falls to pieces at the nonsense of the Israelitish women proposing 'pious orgies' as a way of regaining God's approval and the success in battle which actually follows on that approval. Handel's music follows the text into dullness soon after. Even when he has not been dulled by the words, Handel remains generally at a distance from their intended meanings. The air of the Israelite Simeon, 'Arm, arm, ye brave', is so bloated that it would do for some *miles gloriosus* of the Harapha stamp.

The 1747 word-book of the 'Sacred Drama' was dedicated by Morell to the Duke of Cumberland; 'this faint portraiture of a truly wise, valiant and virtuous commander' was to be taken as an image of the Duke. And retrospectively somewhat exaggerating the fears that Londoners had had of the Jacobites in 1745, Handel's audience took *Judas Maccabaeus* to be a timely tribute to the victor of Culloden. Morell had wanted to make the oratorio even more 'apropos' the Duke's person and exploits, but 'someone', doubtless Handel himself, convinced him that the incidents he planned would make the oratorio too long. 'They were omitted.' Butcher Cumberland, however, still 'made me a handsome present'.

Broughton and Jennens having forced him to divide one kind of liberty from another, Handel was now learning to turn his hand to that political music that Morell was suggesting without feeling that he was touching upon that 'absolute freedom' which Butler had read in the fourth gospel. 'Come ever smiling liberty', 'Liberty, thou choicest treasure', and "Tis Liberty, dear Liberty alone' were received as expressing the general contentment with the state of George II's London.

In the relief at the Pretender's defeat, it was the frantic renewal of 'pleasure' rather than the preservation of 'liberty' that Morell's verses celebrated. Liberty is the companion of 'eternal pleasure' in the first of these airs, the 'source of pleasure' in the second, and the gay comrade of 'lovely life' as they 'with pleasure steal away' in the third. Sung in the intervals of *Hamlet*, hummed along the paths of Vauxhall Gardens where Jonathan Tyers had erected Roubiliac's statue of the composer, whistled by the delivery boys outside Handel's house in Brook Street, these songs of 'Liberty' made Handel more popular than he had ever been. And after the weariness of the public's dismissal of *Hercules* and *Belshazzar* he deserved a pleasant rest from criticism. This puff of patriotic nonsense may have been what his health actually required. Certainly, it did wonders for his bank balance.

Handel agreed to collaborate with Morell again. 'The next year he desired another', the librettist recalled with some pride in 1764, 'and I gave him *Alexander Balus* which follows the history of the foregoing in the *Maccabees.*'

Morell quickly set to work on a version of 1 Maccabees 10:46 – 11:19 which was a little clearer in its outline of history than his *Judas Maccabaeus*, and which, as Handel read the biblical account, might have seemed to promise a chance of distinguishing the characters in a dramatic music. And, with its second round of thumping Jewish victories, the new text offered the likelihood of making some more money. Handel was disappointed on both counts. He made what energetic sense he could of the single moment of real passion when Alexander, setting off to rescue his kidnapped bride Cleopatra, suddenly realizes how fragile his happiness has been, and he produced a poignant meditation on the captivity which expects neither liberty nor liberation in a scene where, after Alexander's death, Cleopatra retreats into a prison of her own sadness. But that was all he found to test his skills. And the oratorio did not make money.

After this dullness it is remarkable that Handel should have retained Morell for *Joshua* in July 1747. *Joshua* begins where *Alexander Balus* left off. Cleopatra had stepped into a life of imprisoning solitude. The Israelites of the new oratorio are discovered at the moment of their release. They have just crossed the river of Jordan; they have entered the Promised Land; they look back for a moment: 'Who can hear of Egypt and not shed a tear?' Handel is always ready with the right sound for such old griefs. The music he writes for the entry into the Promised Land sounds empty, even trivial, beside the song of remembered slavery. He is alerting his hearer to the unsatisfying character of the liberty that the Israelites are celebrating. The Land is not enough. It will not fulfil Handel's idea of a divine Promise. It is, indeed, a land which promises nothing but war.

The angel who appears as they cross into Canaan, 'a sword his hand, a helmet fits his head', is a portent of blood-letting. He looks, says the young Othniel, like a 'hero'. The swords of heroes always prove, in Handel, to be two-edged. The angel describes to Joshua how he is to destroy the king, people, altars, walls of Jericho until there shall be nothing left but ashes blowing in the wind. Joshua responds with a bumptious tune to summon his men: 'Deal death and dreadful war'.

Handel happily accepts Morell's suggestion that love may find a way through all this killing. After the desert, Othniel finds out where 'bleating flocks adorn the plains', and within 'the covert of a friendly shade' he sings to his love. Achsah and he have been taken out of time. The year is always spring for them. Othniel sees around them olive trees, lilies and roses: 'And here we taste true liberty'. This is the fulfilment of the Promise in their lives. But Joshua's trumpet sounds: the war is on them again. The girl's father Caleb, a senile armchair warrior as the music tells us, chases her back into the house and sends the boy off to the front. Caleb talks only of 'fame'.

As it was timeless loving in the garden, so it will be timeless bloodshed. Joshua stops the sun. He wants to kill more enemies before it gets dark. We hear the sun climbing in the first and second violins until, at Joshua's 'Stop', they hold one long extended note. Commentators are divided by the question whether Handel's music for this famous scene evidences 'great imagination and daring' or a condescension to 'the Vulgar Part of his Audience'.[18] The music is both imaginative and vulgar. Handel intends us to hear the sun standing still, and pause ourselves. We are to think for what purpose this cosmic trick has been worked. He gradually takes away each instrumental group from the orchestra and each voice, until we are left alone to contemplate the hidden horror within the chorus's final phrases: 'they yield, they fall, they die'.

After this the Act III opening chorus strikes ironically. Joshua is greeted as the 'great guardian of our liberty!' It is a sad irony that Achsah is now willing to see Joshua as the giver of 'sweet liberty', and Othniel is eager to do Caleb's work when promised the girl as his 'glorious' reward for fighting. Then comes the popular noise of 'See, the conqu'ring hero!', all trumpets and drums. No need now for the divine gift of liberation to the lover. Othniel has it all himself. He is 'godlike', as, triumphal chaplet circling his 'hero's brow divine', he claims Achsah as his due reward. The oratorio ends on the oppressive note of Caleb's attributing all this to Jehovah's 'pow'r supreme'.

His audience did not notice Handel's undermining of the militaristic tone of the old tribal tale. So *Joshua*, like *Judas Maccabaeus*, was popular for all the wrong reasons. Agreeing with Hawkins' judgement that 'See the conqu'ring hero' was not so good as some other choruses he had written, Handel observed wryly: 'You will live to see it is a greater favourite with the people than my other fine things'. Meanwhile he had to get back to his exposition of the liberation which he had come to distinguish as the peculiar gift of God.

The Paradise Garden

Handel had suggested in the most famous air of *Semele* that a capable god would replant the landscape and turn nature into a shaded and flowered garden for his beloved to walk in, and lately he had, in

Alexander Balus, shown, in the kidnapping of Cleopatra from the garden arbour which Alexander had made for her, an image of that brutality in the world which prevents the very possibility of love. These scenes, like the architecture of William Kent, and the paintings of Claude Lorrain, respond to an eighteenth-century interest in reordering the world as a walled garden. Handel had himself seen the most splendid example of such a garden in the Casino built for the Medici in the very centre of Florence. He was rather more insistent than was usual on the scriptural origins of this gardened order. *Semele* and *Alexander Balus* prepare a hearer to receive the wooing of Othniel and Achsah in the garden of *Joshua* as a renewal of the first times of the race. They are dramatizations of Adam and Eve, freely conversing with God as they walk together in the Garden, in the cool of the evening.

In this reference to the Genesis narrative Handel was recapitulating several episodes of his career. The Hamburg theatre had opened in 1678 with Theile's Adam and Eve opera, *Der erschaffene, gefallene, und aufgerichtete Mensch*. Alessandro Scarlatti, Handel's fellow in the 1708 Holy Week project, had the previous Lent presented an oratorio in which a prefatory exegesis of Original Sin led into the actual sin of Cain, *Il primo omicidio*. After Stillingfleet's exuberant account of the divisions of 'Adam' in Levantine mythologies, the deist debates had led from Tindal's dismissal of a silly fable about fig leaves, through Browne's anti-humanist elucidation of *imago Dei*, to Butler's sadly unimaginative statement of how 'an habitual sense of God's presence' might renew in 'such a creature as man' the experience of the first age and the creature again 'walk with God' as in the Garden.[19]

In 1729, the year that Handel was making arrangements for a partnership with Heidegger and scouting for new singers in Italy, the ill-disposed and sarcastic Rolli had observed that 'if everyone were as well satisfied with the company as is the Royal Family, we should have to admit that there never had been such an Opera since Adam and Eve sang Milton's hymns in the Garden of Eden'. Twenty years on, Handel was reconsidering how such an Eden music should sound. And if Jennens and Newburgh Hamilton and Broughton had each resisted the temptation to make an oratorio text from their favourite poet's great work, Handel's dear friend Mrs Delaney (1700–88), wife of the Dean of Down, had not: 'Why, I have made a drama for an oratorio, out of Milton's *Paradise Lost*, to give to Mr Handel to compose to; it has cost me a great deal of thought and contrivance'. Handel did not set her text, though it was more sensitive to Milton's prosody than Hamilton's version of *Samson Agonistes*. He was engaged upon another consideration of the Garden. He was, as he rethought what he had been doing in the garden scenes of *Semele*, *Alexander Balus* and *Joshua*, coming to acknowledge married love as the liveliest human sharing in divine liberty.

His pausing in order to meditate upon the implications of such an acknowledgement, and the theological explorations that it prompted, may be heard in *Solomon* and *Susanna*.

Solomon (1749)

Whoever was the unknown librettist of *Solomon*, there are elements in this next oratorio which make it a companion piece with *Joshua*. It offers a sequence of images of human beings accepting that divine liberation which no one in *Joshua* was ready to receive. Othniel and Achsah had a moment in the Garden but they were seduced out of it. The paradise of innocent married love which they deserted is regained by Solomon and his queen.

That this happens is entirely in the gift of God. This is made very clear at the onset of the oratorio. Solomon, standing in the Temple courtyard, acknowledges the 'gay order' that God creates from the drear confusion of chaos. Handel's sense of the divine order has something of the grace and dancing energy of the order celebrated in Plotinus' *Enneads*. To be a member of this lively harmony, Solomon recognizes, is to live in a garden. Solomon's knowledge of the world is a knowledge of 'each herb and flow'r' not as a botanist knows them, 'the idle pedant' who 'attempts to grasp a name' for his florilegium, but a knowledge of the plants as they exist together within a divine design.

In this world as Garden, Adam walks with Eve. They are wholly in love. The queen has come into her sharing of the delights of the garden world through being linked to the life of Solomon. She has a beautiful serenade of assurance in the happiness of love-making:

> bless'd the day
> On my bosom as he lay
> When he call'd my charms divine
> Vowing only to be mine.

Handel is at last able to make theological sense of the 'circling seasons' of *Athalia*, and the Platonical cycles of *Belshazzar*. He has, like Plotinus, his own way with Platonism. Only in the life with God that is figured in the garden may a human being enjoy the 'one vernal circle' which belongs with timeless love. The royal couple continue in that everlasting spring which Othniel and Achsah had inhabited for a while and which they had abandoned at the temptations of destructive glory and heroic fame. Life, for Solomon and his queen, 'is one perpetual Spring'. The flowers form themselves into fragrant pillows, the zephyrs play about their bed, and nightingales lull them to sleep with their song. But it is not the plants and the birds which make this garden a paradise. The queen is ready to tread 'th' unshelter'd moor' and bear 'burning suns' upon 'the barren plain'; these, too, would be a garden if she shared them with the king. Handel gives an immensely sensual power to her declaration:

> Thy lovely form alone I prize.

The garden is the location of sexual fulfilment.

That this happiness has not been as easily established as such romantic imagery might suggest is hinted for a moment in Solomon's remembrance of the elimination of his elder brother Adonijah, and the assassination of the general Joab in the sanctuary, 'each foe with horror fled'. Solomon has an Othniel past. He has been a sharer in blood-letting. If the idyll of the garden is to be maintained in the way that Handel evidently intends, we may feel that the librettist will have to keep clear of such unpleasant episodes of political history. But why did he not remove these incongruent references to sacrilege and fratricide and murder before handing over the text to Handel? Or how was it, if the librettist could not see how such things spoilt the ideal world he was portraying, that the more sensitive and experienced Handel let them pass? He could as easily have cut these passages as those he cut out of Jennens' *Belshazzar* text. It is sensible to assume that librettist and composer knew their business and understood what they wanted to say in their oratorio. They were perfectly aware that the idyll they were presenting of Solomon and his queen in a recreated garden life must seem to their audience to be wholly removed from contemporary experience. But Handel had been insisting since the start of this great sequence of oratorios with *Hercules* that the gift of such a gracious life was being offered in contemporary Londoners' experience. The killings of Adonijah and Joab represent the actual state of the very world within which the garden has to exist. Solomon's experience comprises both the worst horrors that human beings inflict on one another and the possibility of being freed from such horrors. He is, he knows, a redeemed slave. He has, in his first recitative, acknowledged the 'gracious hand' of God who 'reliev'd Thy slave'. He has been brought by God out of the slavery of blood-letting and anger into the liberation of the garden love with his queen. All this talk of Temple assassinations may not seem to touch very nearly the lives of Handel's London audiences. There were horrendous stories of what went on in the

128

Schloss at Hanover, of course, and some widely repeated anecdotes of the animosity of the King and the Prince of Wales, but references to Adonijah and Joab might seem a curious way to go about making the oratorio and its meaning 'relevant' to Handel's contemporaries. The composer, however, had planned a further step into realism.

At the centre of *Solomon* is the incident of the two prostitutes and the baby. It is a story of the lower reaches of society, of poverty, inadequate housing, sexual exploitation and infant mortality. This sort of thing had been all too apparent to the audience as they made their way to Covent Garden in March 1749. They would also recognize, in their own homes as easily as in the stews of the poor, that meanness of spirit that Handel so unflinchingly presents in his music for the lying prostitute. They would recognize, too, the beauty of the self-sacrifice that he portrays in the song of the true mother. All this is made the more lifelike by Handel's allowing the characters all to speak at once. The trio of Solomon, the mother and the liar is constructed with astonishing dramatic skill. Social worlds collide in this scene as violently as in the streets outside the theatre as the audience had picked their way between beggars. Handel had not attempted anything like this in his operas. Oratorio here enlarges into a realism that anticipates both the noise and the anger of a 'kitchen sink' play. This domestic incident may become as bloody as that of Joab's murder at the altar. The desperate mother has a nightmare vision, presented with terrible poignancy in Handel's air, of the baby being sliced by the soldier's sword, 'the purple tides gushing down his tender sides'. This episode makes it impossible to feel that *Solomon* is dealing with a world removed from our own.

There is a movement from the establishment of the gay order of creation, through the garden loves of the happy pair, and the quarrelling women, into our own experience. Solomon's judgement reaches 'the secret dictates of the human heart' which persist in ourselves now. When the child is put back into her arms, the mother sings of the garden world of the fig tree and the vine, and in her song she, and the shepherd with his maid who figure in her verse, the king surrounded by his courtiers, and the queen in the arbour, are all linked together, and linked with her baby. The song is a lullaby. The idyll is brought home to the prostitute and her child.

The possibility of our sharing such a good life is made even clearer in the third episode of the oratorio. The entry of the queen of Sheba is given such a bustling, public music that it must seem for the length of the symphony that we are about to be taken further from our own personal experience rather than given a more intimate knowledge of the gracious life. But this queen is a figure of ourselves. She comes from a distance and views the gracious garden with a stranger's eye. But she wants to learn what is going on. We are to hear with her the meaning of each 'heavenly strain'. The queen of Sheba is conducted through the Temple and the Palace to the Concert Hall 'where Art her utmost skill displays' and, says the librettist with an encouraging grin, 'claims your praise'.

We realize that we are to hear what the queen of Sheba hears as she hears. We are now in the timeless zone. It is the soloist standing before us who is to sing for the queen of Sheba. It is this very soloist who possesses that voice which she acknowledges to be 'so soft and thrilling'. Solomon commands Handel's orchestra in the pit of the theatre in which we sit. They obey his order to 'sweep, sweep the string'. Solomon will have them play 'th' alternate air' which we see the violinists have ready on their music stands. The chorus on stage is told to spread their voice around our theatre. London theatre and Jerusalem court are one. Just as Handel had proved expert in bringing the theatrical machinery of the transformation scene into the very workings of his opera's plot, so he now makes the conditions of oratorio performance a part of his dramatic presentation. We have been encouraged to accept the singer on the platform, in contemporary evening dress, as Solomon in his court, and now we are being encouraged to see Solomon as our contemporary.

At Solomon's order, his orchestra, which is our orchestra, presents to the queen of Sheba, and to ourselves sitting with her, a sequence of beautifully contrived proofs of the power of music to charm, rouse, beguile and calm her and ourselves. On the close of this wonderful review we are, like the queen of Sheba, to acknowledge the origin of that order which has been manifested in Handel's music: 'Thy harmony's divine'.

Solomon is the mediator of a knowledge, the enabler of a shared experience, for all those who come into this Jerusalem court. And Handel is making an even larger claim for himself than his librettist makes for Solomon. It is through Handel's music that we have been made aware of the divine order. It is an order larger than the theatre in which we have sat to hear the oratorio. It includes not only the royal family in the box, the Jewish merchants smiling that so many Christians have come to applaud yet another of their Hebrew heroes, and middling folk like ourselves, but the harlot's child in the slum tenement, who will never hear his music. It includes as well, that music insists, the young roe, the eagle and the nightingale, the tall palm and the sycamore, the gliding brook, and the rolling surges, all together under the sun, and with the sun under 'an approving smile' of God. The making of such music is itself to be recognized as both the description and the mediation of the Genesis wonder.

From the opening affirmation that it is with harps and cymbals that the Lord is most fitly praised, and that it is with raised voices that his people must declare his wonder to distant nations, through the puns of Solomon in the middle section about 'the uplifted scale' of divine justice, to the queen of Sheba's concert, we have been urged forward to the conclusion that it is in the performance of oratorio that we come nearest to a theological understanding of our experience.

Susanna (1749)

We may, regretfully, agree that political violence, infant mortality and vindictiveness of spirit are recognizable elements of our experience, but is that Garden to be discovered within our world? *Susanna*, which was composed in the same summer and, most probably, to a text prepared by the same sensitive and sympathetic librettist, begins from our experience of unhappiness. There is another of those great choruses of captives which it would seem that Handel needed for his declaration of our ordinary condition before he could start exploring how we may be liberated. The people of this chorus have been driven to the limits of hope. They know that only divine intervention can free them from their oppressors. They are Jewish exiles in Babylon. This scene of captivity is not intended to conjure images of prison doors clanging shut or human beings confined in wire cages or slave labour camps. The exiles are represented, immediately, by a group of prosperous middle-class folk.

The construction of this next sequence was the only major alteration Handel made in the telling of the story he found in the Greek appendix to Daniel. The author of the prophetic narrative at Daniel 13 has no time to do more than mention the names of Joakim and Hilkiah. They are simply put in place as Susanna's husband and father and then forgotten for the duration of the story until they are hauled back into view in the general rejoicing at the end. But Handel needs them both.

He needs the father, now renamed Chelsias, to offer a total reversal of the old armchair warrior Caleb in *Joshua*. Chelsias demonstrates that it is not only the young who can recognize the beauty of the garden life. Caleb had disrupted Othniel and Achsah in the garden, he had kept them apart in the interests of his war policy. Chelsias is there at the beginning of *Susanna* to express his delight in the union of Joacim and Susanna. He is there at the end to praise them as the paradigm couple. Chelsias makes the clearest announcement in the oratorio that what Susanna and Joacim enjoy is offered to every married couple now.

Handel needs Joacim even more. His part in the story is developed so that he shall at various times in the action remind the audience that all this is happening not to a girl alone but to a wife and her husband. Handel brings the husband back into the centre of the music so that we hear how each stage in the attack on his wife is felt in the husband's life. At the start there is a staggeringly beautiful sequence of love lyrics for the pair of them, which offers a history of their courtship and life together. Joacim's charming recollection:

> When first I saw my lovely maid
> Beneath the citron's shade
> In native innocence array'd

is both a delicate gesture of romance and a warning to the audience that Susanna may not be ready to sustain an attack upon the innocent life of the garden. And something of this worry is to be felt again at her response, which is in the more fanciful terms of 'the swain's assiduous care'. This sense of fragility and danger is increased when, having compared their life together to the life of birds in the nest, Joacim announces that he must leave the *nido* for a while. The image then is of the worried parent bird as it forages for the chicks left behind. 'Torments wring her anxious breast, lest some rude hand despoil her nest.' Within this 'lovey-dovey' exchange we may hear the real affection of husband and wife, and the real fears that assault those who seem to have arranged a very comfortable life for themselves. Lest we think that affection a trifling matter, the duet 'When thou art nigh, my pulse beats high' presents a sexuality almost as compelling as in the air of the queen in *Solomon* about the blessed day 'when I was led to ascend the nuptial bed'. *Susanna* is certainly as much an *oratorio erotico* as *Solomon*. Handel is determined to actualize what an audience might make into an idyll if left to themselves.

The eroticism of this scene must, however, be somewhat restrained in order not to create an imbalance in Handel's dramatic design. He needs to be able to show the rougher side of passion in his music for the next scene. Once Joacim has left the garden, we are made aware of the actuality behind the vague fears of the scene between husband and wife. The resonances of primeval times which *Solomon* stirred in the mind are now continued, as in the Genesis narrative itself, in a temptation story. First of all we hear the Fall of the tempters. The First Elder's collapse into unlawful passion is violently portrayed:

> Youth pleads a warrant for his hot desires

> But when the blood should scarce attempt to flow
> I feel the purple torrents fiercely glow.

Sexual passion is deliberately associated by the librettist and the composer with the heroics of the battlefield. The First Elder's blood is responding to a military command to charge upon the enemy:

> When the trumpet sounds to arms
> Will the ling'ring soldier stay?
> When the nymph displays her charms
> Who the call will disobey?

There is a complex irony at work in Handel's music for this air. He had trumpets in his *Susanna* orchestra, but he will not use them here. The Elder is only a soldier in pretence. He is turning Othniel inside out. That young lover wanted to stay with his nymph. He did linger. He obeyed the trumpet only because an old man drove him back to the fight. The First Elder wants to hear a command to assault: he is eager to get into this war. Handel is both declaring the falsity of the Elder's claim to be like the young captain and showing the reality of that violence to which the military trumpet calls the warrior.

So that we continue to associate the garden with the love of husband and wife, Act II begins with the absent Joacim, longing for home, thinking only of Susanna. We next see Susanna herself, in the garden where 'chrystal streams in murmurs flowing' recreate the *Solomon* idyll. Music-making is again the expression of the good life. Susanna's servant-girl sings a serenade that her husband has composed for his wife. Handel took pains to write such a piece as should fit the talent of an amateur musician: 'Ask if yon damask rose be sweet' is a charming trifle. It will not, as the music in Solomon's court was shown to be doing, create an ordered and impregnable world of love. It will not be enough to resist the violence that is coming.

Susanna is confronted with a power that would sweep aside all that she has been given. She resists both the plaintive wooing of the First Elder's 'love-sick strain', and the rapist threats of the Second Elder who would 'force her to bliss'. The da capo form of her refusal is a perfect figure of a virtue that remains unshaken despite temptation and fear. The Elders, however, have the world on their side. They accuse her to the people of having an adulterous meeting with an unknown man.

Joacim, on hearing this accusation, determines to return home at once. He wants to protect her. He means to be a sign of order. But though he composed a song, he is not 'the maker of the world in which she sang'. He does not have the strength to keep the world intact. He does not know how to restore the disrupted garden. Solomon had landscaped his palace grounds, he had presided in his own courtroom, he had conducted his own orchestra. Nothing disturbed him, not even the dispute between the two prostitutes; he could always restore order. But there is no musician-king to sound the divine harmony in *Susanna*. It was with a perfectly steady self-regard that Solomon could pun his way through chaos into wisdom: 'Justice holds the uplifted scale'. The baby was given back to its true mother. When the chorus of *Susanna* looks for justice, it makes a terrible mistake: 'Let Justice reign' in Act II prepares the way for 'Susanna is guilty' in Act III. We are no longer in the landscaped garden. We are out in the wild world. In *Susanna* we confront experience after the Fall.

At this final sequence, we can appreciate how it was Handel positioned the chorus of exiles at the start of this oratorio. Once the Fall has occurred, everyone is an exile. What Handel had intuitively expressed in all those earlier choruses of exiles and prisoners is here located in a theological understanding of humanity under sentence. We are all shut out of the Garden. As at those old Hamburg performances of Theile's *Adam und Eva*, Handel's audience is to recognize 'the creation, the fall, and the sentencing of humanity'. Susanna, oppressed, terrified, in an alien world, is a figure of the race.

Writing *Judas Maccabaeus* in 1747, Handel had insisted on changing the librettist's 'Fallen is the foe' into 'So fall Thy foes, O Lord'. Morell took it that Handel was only interested in a rearrangement of metre, but Handel had effected a momentary removal of attention from the human victory to the theologically resonant sequence of 'fall', 'foe' and 'Lord'. Falling does not simply make the guilty into foes of the Lord. The Fall involves each member of the race. When Susanna understands how she has been trapped by the Elders, Handel enables her to restate the *Judas Maccabaeus* sequence. For her it is a sequence of the 'guiltless' coming to 'death' because the 'innocent' are caught up in 'fall'. The musical emphases occur just where the Halle Pietists discerned the inspirational emphases of the biblical text. This *Susanna* series of emphases introduces another which is resonant of the redemptive acceptance of Gethsemane. 'Blood', 'righteous' and 'heav'n' are brought together in this same aria towards a final prayer of the frightened girl, 'Thy will be done'. 'If guiltless Blood' expresses what he had variously attempted in the *Brockes Passion*, in *Samson* and in *Hercules*. Liberation is not simply the gift of God. It is the gift of God which is received in suffering.

The theological development manifest in Handel's story-tellings, of both mythic and scriptural narratives, originates in his recognition of human beings' need of a freer life, and proceeds through the figuring of that life in scenes of married love in a garden, to the realization that even married lovers are now shut out from Paradise. Our lives are lived in toil and pain and exile. It is in that toil and pain and exile that our need for freedom has to be recognized as a need for the intervention of God.

According to the contemporary orthodox interpretation of the Genesis narrative, the expulsion from the Garden was accompanied by a promise of redemption. The 'proto-evangelion' of Genesis 3:15 was taken to authorize a Christological interpretation of all that followed in the Old Testament. Tindal had recognized the importance of this text and therefore spent so much time making fun of the serpent crawling on his belly. Collins had, equally, made this text the gravamen of his ironic account of Christianity. *Messiah* had itself been received as a fine effort in apologetic response to such underminings of the developing revelation. Handel's willingness to attempt a version of Daniel in *Belshazzar* had placed him at the critical point of contemporary debate about such prophecy. Handel had, however, been somewhat ambivalent about the uses Jennens was making of prophecy in that oratorio. In returning to what was for him a more interesting anecdote of the prophet's career, he was making a more subtle affirmation of prophecy's importance in the divine scheme. *Susanna* declares Daniel to bear a meaning first of all for the prophet's contemporaries, and then for later readers. In the judgement scene, it is to the crowd that the boy makes his immediate appeal. We understand that if we take his message to ourselves we are reinterpreting his words out of their time. Handel is accepting the deist account of how prophecy is read out of the Hebrew texts. He is allowing it to be an occurrence in the creative minds of Christians. But he is also unconcernedly turning this to an orthodox account of what is happening in his oratorio. *Susanna* is announcing itself to be a reconstruction of the scriptural text. The story is becoming in performance a revelation to contemporary audiences. Handel is employing the boy Daniel to affirm the dramatic necessity of a divine intervention if the young woman is to be set free; there must be a god in the machinery. Equally, he is declaring the necessity of such an intervention in our lives if we are to be free.

Handel is making his own way through the confused vocabulary of 'liberty' as 'victory', to a greater understanding of that Pauline announcement which he had rather unthinkingly rolled out towards the end of *Messiah*: 'Thanks be to God who giveth us the victory through our Lord Jesus Christ'. He is ready, in his new understanding, to take the *historie* exampled in the *Brockes Passion* a further step into the lives of his contemporaries. Meaning is to be translated from crucifixion to martyrdom. 'The next I wrote', says Morell, 'was *Theodora* which Mr Handell himself valued more than any Performance of this kind.'

'Far beyond Hallelujahs': *Theodora* (1750)

The legend of Theodora, said to have been martyred at Antioch during the Diocletian persecutions, perhaps about AD 304, had been the subject of a prurient novel by the chemist Robert Boyle: *The Martyrdom of Theodora and Didymus*. Morell based the main body of his libretto on Boyle's novel. He had also read, or been told about, Corneille's *Théodore, Vierge et Martyr*, but he did not find it much to his purpose. The opening scene of the oratorio was entirely his own invention, and he also wrote a lengthy concluding section which he printed in the 1750 word-book. Handel had not found that to his purpose.

Handel chose a subject from the age of martyrs just when an attack was being made against the character of the early Church. Though Toland had accused the Christian communities of the Roman Empire of involvement with the superstitions of contemporary heathendom, and had in this been elaborating notions adumbrated in Burton's *Anatomy of Melancholy* (1621) and Hobbes' *Leviathan* (1651), it was not until 1748, when Conyers Middleton published his *Free Enquiry into the Miraculous Powers* which 'are supposed to have subsisted in the Christian Church from the earliest ages', that the primitive Church's doctrines, hagiographies and ceremonies were systematically aligned with those of paganism. Middleton, with no friendliness towards Catholicism, made it seem that the early Church was exactly like contemporary Rome. Just as pagan. There had never been a holy age of Christianity rejoicing in miraculous healers, inspired scholars and heroic martyrs. It was not only that Middleton refused to credit the miracle stories, which had already been undermined by the publication of Hume's *Essay on Miracles* in April 1748, but that he was declaring 'the history of the Church' to be generally 'fabulous'. Disedifyingly so: 'The lives and characters of the fathers are more likely, in my opinion, to shake a settled, than confirm a wavering faith'.[20]

Leslie Stephen thought that 'Middleton closed the deist controversy' with this challenge to every notion of 'a breach of continuity between sacred and prophane history'.[21] It may be that Browne had not appreciated the peculiar difficulties for orthodox Christian apologetic disclosed by the historical method; that Butler, even if his general approach to theological questions suggests a way of countering those difficulties, had not dealt with them professedly; and that Sherlock, the notorious swimmer, found himself, when attacked by Middleton, quite out of his depth, and unable to do anything to supplement his 1726 argument on *The Use and Intent of Prophecy*. But Handel had been deliberately ignoring all talk of that breach for the whole of his working life. Those who had properly attended to his music had, as early as the revival of *Esther*, realized what he was doing, and had made their fuss. *Messiah* had been the occasion of some robust exchanges on precisely this refusal of the composer to keep his treatments of sacred and profane histories apart. Handel had ever been proposing that his hearers recognize the divinity making itself known within a range of mythic and romantic as well as scriptural histories.

He had been encouraged in this single view of all events by the kind of teaching he had received in the Halle school. The Pietist scholar Gottfried Arnold (1666–1714), in his account of the early Church, *Die Erste Liebe* (1696), had from the very first paragraphs insisted on the likeness of the first Christians and those of later centuries. Each age was an age of miracles. In each age Christians might hear an inner voice calling them forward through the days of their lives to the hour of their deaths. Handel was certainly ready at the end of his career to present the likeness of a martyr of the primitive Church to the members of his oratorio audience. Middleton's *Free Enquiry* appeared at the very end of 1748. *Theodora* was written during the June and July of 1749.

Morell's version of the story begins with the *evangelion* of Diocletian's birthday by Valens, the Roman governor of Antioch. At this good news the citizens are to organize a feast, and offer sacrifice in Jove's temple. Septimus is put in charge of the celebrations, with especial responsibility to punish any who will not take part in the temple ceremony. Didymus, another captain on Valens' staff, appeals for some tolerance to be shown those who hesitate to worship Jove 'yet are friends to Caesar'. Valens cannot acknowledge the distinction. He reinforces his decree with threats of 'racks, gibbets, sword and fire'. Didymus makes an effort to persuade his comrade that coercion must be ineffective in such a matter. Septimus guesses that Didymus himself may be a Christian, but he avoids asking the question. Instead he sets to work on the civilian population. Amongst them, Theodora is already a mistress in 'affliction's school'. In her first air she bids 'adieu!' to the flattering world. Irene, seconding her with observations about 'the vain pomp of proud prosperity', comes very near to suggesting that their Christian faith is the poor man's revenge on the rich. But Irene is rather an 'enthusiast' than a 'leveller'. Septimus goes on

winkling out Christians from 'private oratories' and at last catches up
with the 'rebel' Theodora. She will not have 'worship' characterized as
'rebellion' since it is done in obedience to God's law; so she is carted
off to serve as a sacred prostitute in the temple of Venus. Didymus,
arriving too late to prevent her arrest, rushes off to rescue her.

Valens opens Part II with a festival song for the 'Queen of Love',
coupling her with Diocletian, the hero of 'glory', 'fame' and 'lasting
story'. He delays Theodora's shame, giving her until dusk to make the
demanded offering to Jove. Valens expresses both Boyle's snobbery
and his sniggering in the command that

> The meanest of my guards with lustful joy
> Shall triumph o'er her boasted chastity.

The soldiery themselves, anticipating their night in Venus' temple, are
given even greater brutality to sing:

> While seizing the treasure
> We revel in pleasure,
> Revenge sweet love supplies.

All this *oratorio erotico* stuff was too much for later editors who, as
with the wedded bliss in *Solomon* and *Susanna*, turned versifiers
themselves to supply Handel with a more seemly text.

Theodora in her cell is first tormented by thoughts of her coming
shame, wishing only to be 'embosomed in the grave', and then, contrastingly, inspired with images of 'courts above' to which she will wing
her way like 'the silver dove'. This section of the oratorio is made up
of short scenes which hurry the action along. After Valens in the
drinking hall, and Theodora in the prison cell, we encounter Didymus
and Septimus in the officers' mess. The 'pious youth' admits to being
a Christian, and his friend agrees to assist in the escape plan he has
devised for Theodora. We are taken back for a moment to the hiding-
place of Irene and the Christian womenfolk praying for Theodora.
Then, in her cell again, Didymus offers to deliver her. Theodora,
knowing how risky this would be for him, asks him simply to kill her,
but he insists that they change clothes. She escapes.

Didymus, having become a prisoner in order to release a prisoner,
begins to appreciate dimensions of freedom. In the very first scene he
had asserted a natural right to freedom:

> Ought we not to leave
> The free-born mind of man still ever free?

When Theodora is arrested that general principle is translated into personal action. Didymus determines to 'free the captive fair'. He comes into a further understanding: it is as if he were a Pietist reader being granted a discernment of spirits. His coming to the meaning of 'freedom' is a converting experience. He knows himself better:

> With freedom then
> I will disclose my mind; I am a Christian.

The scene becomes a commentary upon the emphases of John 8:32, 'the truth will make you free', and 2 Corinthians 3:17, 'Where the Spirit of the Lord is, there is freedom'.

By now, Theodora has returned to be greeted by her Christians, but their hymn of thanksgiving is interrupted by the news that Valens has condemned Didymus to die in Theodora's place. His men are now searching the city for her so that she too may be put to death. Hearing that she is not to be shamed in the temple of Venus but to be killed, Theodora determines to give herself up to the Romans. She enters the courtroom just as Valens is sentencing Didymus, and puts herself forward to replace him. Valens, observing that both have pleaded guilty, orders the deaths of both.

We cannot see things quite so clearly. The situation seems full of contradictions. The chorus begins to express something of these contradictions for us in astonishment at the situation of the young people:

> Where each contends
> To fall victorious
> Where virtue its own innocence denies
> And for the vanquish'd the glad victor dies.

In supplying such oxymoronic verse at this critical moment, Morell seems to be hoping that the composer will return to the Baroque world of the old cardinals. But if he did mean to suggest that Handel take up again the ecstatic forms of Roman culture, Morell was unable to relate Theodora to the swooning saints of Baroque devotional imagination. Their sensuality escaped him. His verse has not the confidence of Crashaw's meditations upon the young Teresa of Avila, not yet understanding 'why to show love she should shed blood', and the weeping Magdalen, kissing Jesus' feet in the luxury of 'sweetness so sad, sadness so sweet'. Whatever he hopes to express in Theodora's invocation

> come thou death, thy victim save,
> Kindly embosom'd in the grave,

it is not quite what Donne was managing in his famous declaration to

Christ that he never should be chaste 'except you ravish me'. However, if he had intended *Theodora* to be a representation of such a mystic mystery, Handel would not have needed any very expert prompting from Morell to adopt this religious language. He had returned very cheerfully to this language in the motet *Silete venti*, written at Cannons some time around 1715, perhaps, or even as late as 1726:

> *Dulcis amor, Jesu care*
> *Quis non cupit te amare?*
> *Veni, transfige me.*[22]

Handel is always recouping. In its reversion to some elements of the Roman Baroque, and in so many other ways, *Theodora* represents a culminating expression of what Handel had been attempting to say over a long career.

He had first of all restored the stories of other cultures to that independence which Stillingfleet and his cronies had denied them. He had established, in operas and oratorios, that in their independence they could be heard witnessing to a wonder which is realized in the resurrection Lord. And then, in the process of exploring the myths, he had again made available to the scriptural exegete the 'types' and 'parables' and 'shadows' and 'images' that had so offended Toland when he reviewed the workings of patristic commentary. As Alcestis, Hercules and Semele have become figures of a humanity shared by the hearer, there is an expectation of a similar reference in Saul, Solomon and Susanna. Handel had himself learnt in these retellings that the identification of that reference demanded, however, as careful a thought as in the patristic age. In the course of re-examining that Hebrew Garden narrative, which Tindal had thought so childish, so ready to be put away with the things of 'yesterday', Handel had not found it a simple matter to establish its significance for himself 'today'.

It is certainly possible, as Handel knew, to reinterpret the primeval Garden as a sign of the peculiar blessedness of the Christian in the Kingdom. There were hints of such a reinterpretation already in the Johannine Lord's appearance to the Magdalen as a gardener on Easter morning, in the Pauline image of Christ as the Adam in a new Creation, in the Marcan appreciation of Christian baptism as a sharing in the first days when human beings were at home with angels and wild beasts. And Handel knew more recent versions of this reinterpreting. It occurred in a very popular song that Arnold had written for the Halle Pietists. Arnold's language, as he attached just this resurrection value to the Garden, had been not unlike that of the Roman Baroque to which Morell was now directing the composer's attention:

> The sun shines and the nightingale
> Sings among the leaves and flowers . . .

> There Jesus is the sun, the love,
> The song beside the rising spring . . .

> With him I take my happy walk
> Along the path of Paradise.[23]

Morell still hoped to get away with such a vision of blessedness in a heaven where there are

> Streams of pleasure ever flowing
> Fruits ambrosial ever growing.

Handel himself had, in his eagerness to locate the scriptural announcement of constancy in love being complemented by divine liberation, made quick Garden pairings of Othniel and Achsah, Solomon and his queen, Susanna and Joacim, which had, each in its peculiar way, collapsed under the weight of his typology. By *Theodora*, he was both more intense in his desire to find the appropriate figure and more wary of finding it in a human marrying.

The love of Theodora and Didymus is not going to be consummated in a wedding night. Valens would not allow that in the Antioch gaol; and Theodora is plainly of Paul's opinion that 'she is happier if she remain as she is'. In the resurrection life, 'they neither marry nor are given in marriage'.[24] Marriage is only 'until death do us part', and Handel does not mean us to suppose that Theodora and Didymus are to be parted:

> they are gone
> To prove that love is stronger far than death.

In his talk of love and death, Morell is avoiding the embarrassing puns on 'dying' as sexual intercourse which are scattered through English Baroque poetry. But his lines are certainly related to Crashaw's version of the young Teresa of Avila:

> Scarce hath she blood enough to make
> A guilty sword blush for her sake;
> Yet hath she a heart dare hope to prove
> How much less strong is death than love.[25]

There is a progress in Morell's verse from 'gushing tears' through 'raptur'd soul' and 'love's divinest flame' into 'joys ineffable'. Morell, like Crashaw, would have us apply such language to the union of the Christian with Christ. He is luxuriating in a vocabulary which is only to be fully realized in the enjoyment of a release into divine love. The scene of Didymus in the cell demands a charged verse that shall renew Donne's sense of that release:

> Take me to you, imprison me, for I
> Except you thrall me, never shall be free.[26]

But Morell has not the vitality to speak of such a liberation.

Throughout the oratorio, Irene, the articulatrix of what Morell supposes ordinary Christians should be feeling, has been given a series of pairings in which to fix such proper sentiments. 'Instructed and companioned' in the Christian community, she knows that 'grace and truth' will protect them, 'here and everywhere'; as long as they remain in 'constancy and truth' they will, after 'shame and cruelty', come to 'peace and rest'. Irene prays 'night and day' that Theodora may be 'ever calm and ever pure'. 'Liberty and life' trips as easily as the others off her tongue. It is as familiarly used in the automatic pairing of 'liberty and life' by Septimus, in his air 'Dread fruits of Christian folly', by the chorus, in 'Blest be the hand', and by Theodora herself, in the recitative 'Ah! what is liberty or life to me?' But when Irene, humanely aware of something of the cost the two young people are paying, sings admiringly of Theodora's 'disdaining liberty and life', Handel wants to make a distinction. He allows us to hear both her sympathetic sense of the prison cell and the executioner, and her inability to appreciate that the martyr is not disdaining liberty but surrendering life in order to be liberated. The tone of Handel's presentation of the Christians' deaths is just that of one of the earliest Baroque poems in English, Southwell's *St Peters Complaint* in which the old saint longs for the happy death of the young martyrs:

> Rue not their death whom death did but revive;
> Yield ruth to me that lived to die alive.

Handel is as aware as the Baroque poet of an oxymoron at the centre of human experience. His music represents the martyr as dying to be free.

That Christian freedom which is the complement to the constant love of God to which a martyr witnesses is not properly figured as Irene's 'peace and rest' or the release from 'Bondage', 'burden' and 'yoke' of the earlier oratorios. It has to be figured in a renewal of redeemed life. It is just at the point where the hearer is made aware of Didymus being at once the prisoner in the cell and the sharer in a truth that makes free, that Handel places the great resurrection chorus 'He saw the lovely youth'.

Handel's splendid music demands that we wholly attend to the miracle story of Luke 7:11–17:

> He saw the lovely youth, death's early prey,
> Alas! too early snatched away;
> He heard his mother's funeral cries:
> Rise youth, he said; the youth begins to rise,
> Lowly the matron bowed, and bore away the prize.

The narrative of Jesus seeing the 'lovely youth' comes home to the audience as having a precise reference to the one who has already been identified as 'excellent youth', 'pious youth' and 'generous youth', to Didymus. The Lucan miracle story is to shape our appreciation of Didymus' experience. He is to come through a death to a resurrection. The chorus provides the interpretative key by which the irrational terrors of a world in which men martyr men will be opened upon an intelligible divine order. The Maddalena of his early *Resurrezione* oratorio had not been able to express the life she felt within her heart. Handel has now found the music for this mystery. No wonder, as he told Morell, that he valued this music 'far beyond' the 'Hallelujahs' of *Messiah*.

This significant chorus shifted attention from Theodora to Didymus. He takes her place in Handel's design just as he takes her place in Valens' prison. Whilst we might comfort ourselves with the thought that Theodora is a fanatic, we cannot easily put Didymus aside. The interest of the musical structure within which Handel places the young captain prompts our self-consideration as members of a reasonable race. If we are quite willing to affirm with Didymus that we 'neither hate nor scorn' life here and now, we have to ask ourselves whether we should not also make our own this reasonable chap's appreciation of martyrdom. For *Theodora* has developed into a thoroughgoing denial of the deistical assertion that the essentials of Christianity are discernible in every religion, savage, classical or modern. Through his musical characterization of Didymus, Handel is affirming that there is, whatever the deists have been saying, a peculiar Christian mystery, and it is not as old as creation. Nor is it a generalizable member of Ramsay's 'three State' thesis of Creation, Fall and Hero. It is a mystery of martyrdom and liberation through the singular vitality of Easter. 'Rise youth, he said.'

Theodora constituted a challenge to the way in which those who had been buying tickets for the oratorios usually looked at life. It was not a commercial success: only three poorly attended performances in 1750 itself, and not another until the single performance of 1755. 'The Jews will not come to it', Handel remarked after the second performance, 'because it is a Christian story; and the ladies will not come, because it is a virtuous one.' But it was a tremendous personal achievement.

In his previous oratorios Handel had been moving to fulfil the programme inherent in Butler's affirmation of 'a state of absolute freedom in the most literal and proper sense'. Through this 'Christian story', Handel had come near to making a convincing announcement of that 'entire coincidence of our wills with the will of God' in which Butler had known our absolute freedom to consist. In considering that coincidence of human with divine will, Butler had had to content himself with the cautious qualifier, 'whether attainable in this world or not'.[27] He did not look hopefully for that reversal of human will which should free the Indian and the Negro. Handel, however, proceeded to declare his own sense of the liberty of the children of God in a way that, most dramatically, reversed the judgement of his contemporaries.

Notes

1 Cf. E. Bredenfoerder, *Die Texte der Händel-Oratorien* (Leipzig, 1934). It was Schieferdecker (1679–1732) who married Buxtehude's daughter and got the organist's job at Lübeck in 1707.

2 J. Butler, *Works*, ed. W.E. Gladstone (2 vols; 1896), *Analogy*, Part I, ch. 2, para. 12.

3 Ernst Bloch, *Zur Philosophie der Musik* (Frankfurt, 1974), trans. P. Palmer as *Essays on the Philosophy of Music* (1985), p. 8.

4 M. Tindal, *Christianity as Old as the Creation, or, The Gospel a Republication of the Religion of Nature* (1730), pp. 257–8.

5 Cf. F.M. Krouse, *Milton's Samson and the Christian Tradition* (New York, 1974).

6 See discussion in W. Dean, *Handel's Dramatic Oratorios and Masques* (1959), p. 370, referring to A. Heuss, 'Das Semel-Problem bei Congreve und Händel', *Zeitschrift der Internationalen Musikgesellschaft* (1914).

7 E. Stillingfleet, *Origines Sacrae, or a Rational Account of the Grounds of Natural and Revealed Religion* (1662) II, p. 157.

8 J.A. Freylinghausen, *Geistreiches Gesangbuch* (Halle, 1705), no. 66.

9 Cf. D.C. Allen, 'Milton and the descent to light', *Journal of English and German Philology* 60 (1961) and M.Y. Hughes, 'The Arthurs of the *Faerie Queene*', *Études anglaises* 6 (1953); on the question of the relation

of mythic hero and Christ, cf. H. Rahner, *Griechische Mythen in christlicher Deutung* (Zürich, 1957); H. F. G. Swanston, *Language for Madness* (1976).

10 T. Broughton, *Christianity distinct from the Religion of Nature* (1732) I, pp. vi and 3.

11 *Ibid.*, II, p. 40.

12 T. Broughton, *Bibliotheca historico-sacra* (2 vols; 1737, 1739) II, p. 528; I, pp. 539–40; II, p. 548.

13 *Ibid.*, I, p. 320; II, pp. 545, 103–4, 202–3.

14 Broughton, *Christianity distinct* I, pp. 12–15.

15 Broughton, *Bibliotheca* I, pp. 62, 112, 551 and 484.

16 Dean, *op. cit.*, p. 471.

17 Cf. Butler, *ed. cit.*, *Analogy*, Part II, vii, 52 and 53.

18 Cf. Dean, *op. cit.*, p. 501, and, contrastingly, C. Avison, *Essay on Musical Expression* (1752), cited Dean, *op. cit.*, p. 502.

19 Cf. Butler, *ed. cit.*, *XV Sermons*, xiv, 7.

20 C. Middleton, *Free Enquiry into the Miraculous Powers* (1748), p. 162.

21 L. Stephen, *English Thought in the Eighteenth Century* (1876) I, p. 269.

22 Cf. R. Myers, *Handel's Messiah, a Touchstone of Taste* (New York, 1948), p. 85.

23 G. Arnold, *Gottliche Liebes-Funcken* (repr. Frankfurt, 1968), no. 87.

24 1 Corinthians 7:40; Matthew 23:30; cf. Mark 12:25, and Luke 20:35.

25 R. Crashaw, 'A Hymn to the Name and Honour of the Admirable Saint Teresa'; cf. H. F. G. Swanston, 'The Baroque element in *Troilus and Cressida*', *Durham University Journal* XIX, no. 1 (1957), pp. 14–23, and 'The Second Temple', *ibid.*, XXV, no. 1 (1963), pp. 14–22.

26 J. Donne, *Holy Sonnets*, 'Batter my heart, three-person'd God'.

27 Butler, *ed. cit.*, *VI Sermons*, iii, para. 3.

4

Virgo as sign of
resurrection life, 1752

Whilst Handel had been composing *Theodora*, the most famous of
contemporary apologists for resurrection doctrine had again been
occupying headlines. Thomas Sherlock, who had published his *Trial
of the Witnesses* in 1730, was now bishop of London. His short book
had purported to pass judgement on the evidence provided by the
evangelists and their informants of the several resurrection appearances of Christ. After some rather biased examination, these witnesses
were satisfactorily cleared from the imputation of impious fraud made
against them. Christ was proven to have risen. This litigious tract had
been twice reprinted in 1748. In 1749, however, Sherlock was having
a rather noisier lawsuit in Handel's own parish. He was disputing the
patronage of St George's, Hanover Square with the archbishop of
Canterbury. The composer was regular in his attendance at this
church, 'expressing by his looks and gesticulations the utmost fervour
of devotion'. Perhaps Sherlock's noise was a factor in Handel's taking
up again his livelier considerations of what resurrection might mean
for Christians. Another, certainly, was a rather prestigious invitation,
in December 1749, to provide music for a great new spectacle at
Covent Garden.

Tobias Smollett (1721–71) had written an *Alceste* and Rich, the
manager of the theatre, had plans for stupendous scenery, wonderful
singers and grand music. Handel must have been much attracted by
a scheme which promised so lavish a context for his music with absolutely no financial risk to himself. He was not asked to provide music
for Hercules, Admetus or Alcestis. These were speaking parts, for
Smollett was determined to control the shape of the whole enterprise.

But he wrote a great bass aria for Charon as he gondoliered the dead across to Hades, and a welcoming chorus when Hercules brings Alcestis back.

Any return to this heroic story must bring with it remembrances of those typological connections of Hercules and Samson and the Lord of *La Resurrezione*; and of the many different contexts in which Handel had worked out these connections since he first found Keiser's 1699 *Hercules* in the cupboards of the Gänsemarkt theatre. This 1749 *Alceste* is certainly a splendid celebration of Hercules as a prefigure of the rising Christ of Easter:

> Fiends, Furies, Gods, all yield to thee,
> and Death hath set his captive free.
> All hail, thou mighty son of Jove!
> how great thy pow'r! how great thy love!

But there is only this fragmentary music as a hint of what Handel was suggesting for the future of this kind of mythologization in Christian thought. Smollett's project was abandoned, and although in 1750 Handel frugally re-employed the music, he could not bring himself to be interested in the poor little allegory of *The Choice of Hercules* between Pleasure and Virtue that Morell had cobbled together.

He needed a libretto which would allow him to go further in a retelling of stories which should take account of the resurrection life revealed in Christ. He gave a clearer indication of what he was proposing in the *Jephtha* of 1752.

Jephtha, too, is a recoupment of an earlier moment in Handel's career. Jennens' prefatory note to *Saul* had acknowledged that some elements of his design, notably the character of Merab, had been adopted from Abraham Cowley's *Davideis* of 1650. In turning to the story in Judges 10 – 11, Handel is fulfilling the last of Cowley's hopes for a Christian drama. The 1650 preface to his unfinished David epic had urged Cowley's successors to continue his effort to make the scriptural characters more readily available to English readers: 'Why will not the actions of Sampson afford as plentiful matters as the Labors of Hercules? why is not Jephthah's Daughter as good a woman as Iphigeneia? and the friendship of David and Jonathan more worthy celebration than that of Theseus and Perithous?'[1] Cowley had attacked 'senseless *Fables* and *Metamorphoses*' in his attempt to erect the Scriptures as the proper subject for epic and tragedy. Handel had been generous enough to do both sorts of work. After *Samson* and *Hercules* and *Saul* and *Teseo*, he was now to reconsider Jephthah's daughter.

The choice of the myth of Hercules' rescue of Alcestis for some development as a resurrection story was evidently the easy option. Handel was much braver in scriptural story-telling. The narrative collected in Judges is not purpose-built for such a resurrection exegesis. The Jephthah story, which has links not only with Greek tales of Idomeneus and Agamemnon but, through Levantine memories, with a body of Mesopotamian lore about gods, old men, the generation gap, and bearers of good news, is an uncomplicated story of tribal custom. The Israelites, having been punished by successive defeats by the Ammonites, abandon the gods who have failed them and return to the worship of the Lord. They choose an outlaw, Jephthah, to lead them and, to ensure success, he vows that on returning victorious he will sacrifice whoever first greets him at his door. Jephthah wins the battle. 'And behold his daughter came out to meet him with timbrels and with dances; she was his only child.' She has ruined any hope he had of grandsons. After a two-month stay among the women of the tribe, the virgin was sacrificed. 'And it became the custom in Israel that the daughters of Israel went year by year to lament the daughter of Jephthah the Gileadite four days in the year.'[2]

This is a horrid story. It places an inexorable terror at the heart of the relations of human beings with God. Tindal thought that its horror reverberated through Christian history. It may not have seemed very significant to the Jews 'that a single Person in the Power of another might be devoted to God', since 'free and independent Nations were so devoted' at the close of their campaigns. But, by some perverted reading of Jephthah's story in Hebrews, it now appears that 'putting innocent and conscientious Men to Death on account of Religion' has become a common horror of Western culture. To Tindal, the story of Jephthah had a terrible relevance 'even at this Day'.[3]

The oratorio begins with the inexorable: 'It must be so'. But there are other phrases of this first choral entry in which Handel finds a contrary emphasis: 'ourselves must choose' and 'no more'. There is evidently to be a debate; and a debate which will not be muddled by anything like King's speculations about 'predestination'. When Jephtha himself links the determinist catchphrase, 'It must be so', with the determination of God, the chorus is ready to second him. Morell's text for their great music, 'How dark, O Lord, are Thy decrees', had reached a similar linking conclusion: 'What God ordains is right'. The composer threw this out, replacing it with that tag from Pope's versification of Bolingbroke's deist morality: 'Whatever is, is right'. He then prised the two halves of the line apart: 'Whatever is' receives the complex music of differing voices proper to the complexities of existence. Between this and the next phrase Handel interposes a tripping measure that mocks the simplistic unison shout of 'is right'. The shout gets louder and is blown up in the accompaniment but Handel has seen to it that we are not going to be impressed by the clamour of determinism.

His design for the oratorio's shape is itself a rebuttal of inevitability. As in *Theodora*, Handel organizes a late shift of attention from the title role to another character who can better bear his meaning. In *Jephtha* we get away from the judge, the 'glorious conqueror', and his self-regarding rhetoric, and turn to his daughter. Jephtha's vow occurs in the course of an unremarkable recitative. But what happens to his daughter in this retelling is a staggering declaration that reversal of human understanding, conventional law and authoritative Scripture is possible in our relations with God. As the chorus sings 'How dark, O Lord', night is passing. In the morning, Jephtha, it seems, is still interested only in 'a father's woe'. But as the sun rises, even Jephtha is brought for a moment to attend to his daughter. Then he retires from the action. He has only a couple more phrases to sing. His daughter is already effecting a translation from 'my father's will' to 'the call of heaven'. Determinism is re-known as vocation. Handel, like Butler, is maintaining that 'whatever is', in order to be 'right', has to undergo conversion into membership of an order.

He has shown, in the 'bright cherub' of *Susanna*, that this order, as in Butler's story of Balaam and his favourite epistle, Hebrews, reaches to angels. Theodora had sighted an 'ever-singing, ever-loving choir' in the courts of heaven. Now, in *Jephtha*, first an army of 'aetherial origin' fights Israel's battles, then an angel descends in the *machina* to prevent the human sacrifice, to reinterpret the old man's vow, and to declare the true character of the order which God is offering to humanity.

This irruption of the angelic messenger recalls those sudden changes of plotting, descents of divinities, and happy endings which are conventional in *opera seria*. It is, perhaps, an echo of the Abraham and Isaac story of child-sacrifice. Or, since Morell kept Abbé Pellegrin's invention of 'Iphise' as the name for the judge's daughter, this incident may have some forerunner in Artemis' substitution of the girl by a sacrificial kid in Euripides' *Iphigeneia in Aulis*. Handel has greater surprises yet for those, Jewish as well as Christian, who have settled for themselves all questions of the biblical text and its sacred inalterability. Like Butler, again, Handel was ready to affront those 'and there are at least more of them than have a right to claim such superiority', who 'take for granted that they are acquainted with everything', and who think no subject, if properly treated, 'can be treated in any manner but what is familiar and easy to them'.[4]

The Judges narrator had stressed the girl's virginity at her death as the most regrettable feature of the situation. That she would never be a mother had been a disgrace added to the terrors of death. Other librettists and composers had accepted the death of the girl as the climax of their versions of the tale. Morell had read the *Jephtes sive Votum* of George Buchanan (1506–82), and the Pellegrin *Jephté* that Michel de Montéclair (1667–1737) had made into a notorious *tragédie lyrique* in 1736. Handel may have known *Il sagrifizio di Gefta* by Giuseppe Porsile. He was certainly acquainted with Maurice Greene's English *Jephthah* of 1737. He had studied Carissimi's Latin *Jephte*, written before 1650. All these had placed the vow and its fulfilment in human sacrifice at the centre of their designs. But, though he much admired Carissimi's climactic 'Ploratae filiae', Handel felt entirely free to make his own revision of the story. Handel's angel does not simply stop the human sacrifice; he consecrates the girl as a virgin in the service of God. She is to live 'in pure and virgin state for ever'. Handel's audience is to hear the vocation of virginity given to Jephtha's daughter as 'freedom to the slave'.

His eyes were so tired that he stopped work for eleven days after setting the first two lines of 'How dark, O Lord', and he had to stop work again, after a further four days' work. When he began again, four months later, he had sight in one eye only. He was totally blind by the spring of 1753. He marked these terrible interruptions with some marginal notes in his native German, which he had not used for a long time, even in his letters to Michaelsen. It was now the language in which he talked to himself. Handel's personal apprehension of a wonder in the girl's virginity is most affectingly revealed in his music as he declares that her presence in the world will be 'sweet as sight to the blind'. Her continuing virginal presence is at the climax of the music drama.

Morell evidently saw virginity through rosy spectacles, all sweetness and 'blest angels'. In his text, the girl's relations behave rather as if she were a novice taking the veil at the local convent. Her uncle congratulates her father, the judge, on his daughter's vocation; her mother babbles about 'submissive joy'; and, to grace the scene with a little sentimental sadness, her discarded lover talks of 'so dear a loss' as she wishes him happiness with some other girl. Handel would have heard such pious nonsense about nuns from the Italian singers with whom he worked for so much of his career. It was the sort of notion they would have retained from their Catholic childhoods. Even if he had not learnt something of the more hard-working reality of the nun's life during his years in Rome, Handel could not have been content with Morell's version of cloistered virginity.

Morell's usefulness lay not in his own feeble experiments in esoteric versification but in his capacity to prompt Handel to energetic renewal of some element in his past experience. He responds now to the 'incessant pangs' of the 'raptured soul' that is 'panting for liberty'. And, most dramatically, to 'virgin'.

Contemplating this new text, Handel recollected, more vividly than when he was working on *Theodora*, the devotional vigour of the Baroque culture. He had once, in a society that was excited by Bernini's languishing sculptures, Pietro da Cortona's gesticulating ceiling and Crashaw's ecstatic verses, gained the reputation, as Cardinal Pamphilj declared in his *novello Orfeo* tribute, for *soave armonia* and *grata melodia*. Handel enjoyed the memory of that reputation. His last London offering was yet another version, suitably fattened for the English market, of Pamphilj's *Trionfo del Tempo e del Disinganno*.

He was certainly thinking, as he put the *Jephtha* music together, of celebrations of the Roman liturgy. In hopes of lighting upon some stimulating phrases that would give him the tone for what Winton Dean rightly esteems as 'the profoundest spiritual statement of his artistic life',[5] he was turning over a collection of masses by Frantisek Habermann (1706–83). He found starting-places for *Jephtha* airs and choruses in *Kyrie*, *Gloria*, *Osanna* and *Agnus Dei*.

It is likely, at such prompting, that he recalled his own share in Roman celebrations. His search for the proper music for the 'pure and virgin state' of Jephtha's daughter would have reminded him of his hymns for the enheavened Virgin, 'Donna che in ciel', perhaps, or 'O del ciel Maria Regina'. Prince Ferdinando, reminiscing after the funeral of poor dropsical Francesco Maria de' Medici, seems to have misattributed to Handel a characteristically Baroque contemplation of the weeping Madonna, *Il Pianto di Maria*. But there is no doubting that Handel is the composer of the 1707 *Salve Regina* for Ruspoli. His music for this hymn to Mary if not recognized by every critic as an act of 'chivalrous devotion', declaring 'something mystic, dark, and gripping', sounds, even to less sympathetic ears, as 'the apotheosis of these Romish compositions', too warmly exhibiting 'the more sentimental aspects of Mediterranean Catholicism'.[6] The Virgin, Queen of Heaven, is hailed in this hymn as the protectress of those 'poor, banished children of Eve', shut out from the Garden, whose life is 'mourning and weeping' in a world of tears, as our 'most gracious advocate' in the courtroom of divine justice, and as the lady who will, 'after this our exile', show us her Son.

If virginity were indeed associated in Handel's imagination with such a care for those who had been shut out from the shared happiness of the Garden, such a consolation for the mourner and the exile, such a pleading for the accused, and such an invitation to the presence of Christ, then he would certainly have received a virgin as the probable figure of a reversal not only of the distress of Iole, the exile of Israel, the mistrial of Susanna, but of the misery of the Indian and the Negro.

In the *Salve Regina*, especially in his setting of 'suspiramus', there had been something of the emotional intensity of those 'incessant pangs' which Morell had associated with 'rapturous soul'. Handel had also in his Roman years been sensitive to a 'panting for liberty'. He had heard a more liturgical music which linked the Virgin with the relief of the oppressed when he went to hear his antiphons *Haec est regina virginum* and *Te decus virginem* at the Vespers for the feast of Our Lady of Mount Carmel commissioned by Cardinal Colonna in 1707. His antiphons and psalm settings had been followed by a plainchant *Magnificat*. That canticle gives an effective energy to the hope expressed in the sighings of the *Salve Regina*. The Virgin declares that God will fulfil his promise to the weak. These verses proved to have a recurring attraction for the composer. He made an English music for 'I will magnify Thee, O Lord' for Chandos in 1717, and another for the Chapel Royal in 1724.

Morell's texts for his last two oratorios prompted Handel to consider the particular reference of virginity to what he had been discovering of our leaning on God, of liberty, and of resurrection life. He contemplated again that pairing of images of a virgin as sharer of sorrows in a terrifying world and as signaller of divine liberation from those sorrows. In *Theodora*, the virgin had been at risk. Imprisoned, threatened with violation and a shameful death, she had been a figure of our fragility. When he came to declare the effectiveness of divine power, Handel turned attention from the virgin to the gracious youth. In *Jephtha*, the virgin is herself the bearer of resurrection vitality. At the crisis of this oratorio an angel descends to ensure that we appreciate a connection of the 'virgin state' with 'faith' through an inspiration of 'the Holy Spirit'. By faith, the virgin comes into new life with her community. The daughter of the Old Testament judge is now identifiable as a member of that order announced in a clutch of New Testament resurrection stories. She is Jairus' daughter, given back from the dead to her parents. Coming 'safe from the grave', she is greeted as a sign of 'the life of heav'n'.

The discernment of such an association of Jephtha's daughter with 'Talitha cumi' is just the sort of experience that Francke had identified as the evangelical *Durchbruch* or breakthrough. Handel had broken through the literal text to discover for himself and for others 'a foretaste of resurrection'. From this, the oratorio races into a sequence of 'glad songs' to celebrate the virgin's significance to the community. The *lieto fine* is a dance begun by the virgin which embraces each of the characters until they are all singing of their being 'freed' by God to enjoy a new 'peace'. By a nice turn of Morell's language, this *Magnificat* delight in 'Heaven's all-ruling power' is said to check 'the rising sigh' of *Salve Regina*. Having prevented the deistical determinism of 'It must be so' being translated into 'What God ordains', Handel can complete his reversal of Morell's opening phrase by a praising emphasis upon 'So be it'. The oratorio ends upon 'Hallelujah' and 'Amen'.

The audience is now to see in Jephtha's daughter an image of their own inability to save themselves and a promise of their own participation in resurrection. The suggestion to decent Georgian couples on their evening out that they should receive a consecrated virgin as the sign of what they were themselves called to be might have seemed odd, and indeed, affronting; especially to those who recognized that Handel had reversed the plot and tenor of the biblical narrative. But, at the close of Handel's career, things were not as they had been when he started. He had established that his dramatic story-tellings should assist in the development of theological understanding. In *Jephtha* he was bringing his hearers to realize that there was a resurrection life beyond the aridities of Woolston's two-pronged attack in his *Six Discourses* on the character of the Virgin and the credibility of Jesus' resurrection miracles;[7] beyond the dull orthodox responses of Bishop Richard Smalbroke (1672–1749) in a *Vindication of the Miracles of our Blessed Saviour* (1729–31), and Bishop Zachary Pearce (1690–1774) in *Miracles of Jesus Vindicated* (1729). Beyond, even, the famous knock-down argument of Bishop Sherlock's *Trial of the Witnesses*, which had been reprinted thirteen times since its publication in 1730. *Jephtha* did not put an immediate stop to such unhelpful distractions. Sherlock's piece was reprinted again in 1830. But there were at last, after so many operas and oratorios, divines who could accommodate such a rereading and retelling of Judges. They had learnt something about stories.

Morell himself is, perhaps, too special a case, but in 1752, the year of *Jephtha*, Robert Lowth (1710–87), from whose verses Morell had made *The Choice of Hercules*, was, in Oxford lectures *de sacra poesi hebraeorum*, making the first effort by a theologian of the Georgian Establishment to say something about the literary forms of the Bible. That same year, too, the more popular, latitudinarian Conyers Middleton abandoned his controversy with Sherlock to write an essay on 'The Allegorical and Literal Interpretation of the Creation and Fall of Man', in which he employed distinctions familiar in Handel's opera houses. In dealing with the scriptural stories, Middleton, whilst preferring those that present truth 'under the veil of fiction' to those that pretend to being 'real history', is, like Handel, most excited by a story; Job is his instance, which 'breathes a dramatic and fabulous air'. He recognizes in his reading of Scripture what Handel had been exampling in Opera and Oratorio. Whether a story be a 'Poetic Drama', a 'History', or a 'Fable', it may be 'exactly the same with regard to its effect and influence in Christianity'.[8]

As Handel performs his last oratorio, it is becoming apparent to others that an Old Testament story may be retold as a myth of present Christian liberation.

Notes

1   A. Cowley, *Davideis* (1656), Preface; A. R. Alker (ed.), *Works* (1906) I, pp. 13–14.

2   Judges 11:34b and 39b–40.

3   M. Tindal, *Christianity as Old as the Creation, or, The Gospel a Republication of the Religion of Nature* (1730), pp. 97–8.

4   J. Butler, *Works*, ed. W. E. Gladstone (2 vols; 1896), *XV Sermons*, Preface, 2.

5   W. Dean, *Handel's Dramatic Oratorios and Masques* (1959), p. 592.

6   Cf. with P. M. Young, *Handel* (1946) and H. C. Robbins Landon, *Handel and his World* (1984), A. C. Bell, *Handel before England* (1975), p. 33, and B. Lam, 'The church music' in *Handel, a Symposium*, ed. G. Abraham (1954), p. 160. A contrary use of 'sentimental' occurs in the *Universal Chronicle* obituary (21 April 1759), which speaks of Handel's composing in 'a Sentimental language rather than mere sounds'.

7   For a discussion of the resurrection reference of such miracle stories, cf. H. F. G. Swanston, *The Community Witness* (1967).

8   C. Middleton, *Works* (1752) II, pp. 131–3.

Index